Edited by Caryn Mirriam-Goldberg
Woodley Press editor Kevin Rabas

Copyright 2011 Woodley Press
All rights reserved
Printed by Lightning Source
Cover Photo by Stephen Locke
Cover and book design by Leah Sewell and Matthew Porubsky
Copy Editor: Michael D. Graves

Woodley Press
Department of English
Washburn University
Topeka, KS 66621
http://www.washburn.edu/reference/woodley-press/

ISBN: 9780-9828752-5-4

other recent titles available from **Woodley Press**

Ghost Stories of the New West:
From Einstein's Brain to Geronimo's Boots
    Denise Low

Fire Mobile (the pregnancy sonnets)
    Matthew Porubsky

Kansas Poems
    William Stafford edited by Denise Low

Sky Land
    Michael Johnson

Finding the Edge
    Al Ortolani

Begin Again

150 Kansas Poems

Edited by Caryn Mirriam-Goldberg

WOODLEY PRESS

Celebrate This Kansas

Celebrate this sky, this land beyond the measured time
that tilts the seasonal light. Dream the return of the stars,
the searing rise of heat or fall of storm crossing through
the secret-holding cedars and witness rocks for thousands of years.
This air we breathe belonged to those who spoke languages forgotten
as the glaciers cusping the ridges. These fields we walk once rushed
in ocean long after, long before what we know as mapped time.
This rain was once a man's last breath, this heat what warmed
a weathered rock enough for a woman to rest on with her baby,
these fossils once love songs of memory and longing after the beloveds die.
Everything we know of Kansas comes from this: rivers aching east
after scouting out and winding their mark through the horizons of grass,
skies mirroring orange to black, moon to sun, hail to pale breeze,
ready to give everything to us like any true heart.
All we see, the ghost and angel of the land's lightest touch,
a trail through the prairie, a hard rain in the woods -- beyond naming
and yet named Step into where you already are, where once
the grandmothers and grandfathers sang out their stories of
weather and loss, wars and births. The bones of this land and the feathers
of this sky compose this Kansas that knows us better than we know ourselves,
that is always ready with wind, shimmer, falling grasses and stone roots
to show us what it means to live where the earth and stars converge.

    -- Caryn Mirriam-Goldberg

(written for the Kansas Susquicentennial Celebration, 1/29/11)

Contents

Summer

Autumn

Winter

Begin Again

Getting There

Maybe you had to be there
or more likely wanted to.
It was possibly vital
a goal or destination
that might have had
unerring potential.

Maybe you made elaborate plans
what to take and how much.
You could have just gone as you were.
You are pretty sure your
arrival would have been
important to somebody.

Maybe trust could have been saved
a fence made true
or a contract signed because
you got there whether
puffing and blowing desperation
or gracefully early.

Maybe you were chosen
an omen set your path.
Maybe you took a desire
seriously getting there
far ahead of yourself.

Maybe there won't turn
out to be like you
think it is. Maybe it
ought to shift for itself
with you right here
breathing down to the
hairs of your body.

I Carry Three Birds

Their wings rub against my ribcage,
trapped, and each heart pounds fast,
as if I've stopped some kind of migration.
The cardinal knows when to save with a song,
when to fly and when to nurture.
The second is a robin, for singing during the afternoon
when my thinking can be confusing, when I mistake
the danger of branches for the opportunity of building.
And the last is the crow, for protection, for remaining when it's cold.
But I confuse which bird I need
with the one I listen to, my mistake
in switching them around.
Sometimes the singing should continue,
but I crow curses instead.
Sometimes when I should let go
to soar, I scamper within the trees.
Even then, all three continue
to build a nest out of the ruins,
to nestle in through my winters.

Robins Keep Their Secrets

Suppose for a moment
they do not migrate south
for the winter as everyone assumes

but instead don black hoods
and abandon leaf strewn lawns
for the white freedom of December skies.

Were you to look just so
you might see flocks of them
flashing their fiery badges

where the sun has barely cleared
the tops of distant trees.
And were you walking in the woods,

where ice is just beginning
to skim the creek that's pooling
behind the fallen sycamores and oaks,

if you listened, you might hear them
scratching in the bracken,
see their shadows mirrored

in the surface of the stream
as they bow to drink
at the swifter narrow sluices.

winter solstice song

winter solstice song:
love can not cure loneliness
loneliness is love

all things sheathed in ice
a sough issues from each blade
aching to decide

absolute zero
one spark rings then another
autonomous joy

walking through winter
her emptiness emerges
to carry my heart

steel sky descending
engaged in stainless quiet
a kernel of love

woken by a flash
pre-dawn thunder & big snow
eerie new year's eve

one one of one one
will i be alone this year
will i be all one

one one of one one
a bond to our calender
or to emptiness!

she was the archer
who struck my heart & quickened
grace to be reborn
again we have died
& the secret arrows fly
etching this arcade

the sky is a tongue
a vulgate palimpsest wrought
anew by each choice

what have i written
the flotsam of long short days
shortly growing long
the milkyway smiles
you are your own galaxy
a kind glacial truth

charlie mingus plays
spurring the indifferent stars
to forbidden song

able to respond
he finds himself a star
in the winter sky

Inside the Snow Globe

At long last you are in
the blizzard behind glass,
this trail of flakes your cape
of disappearance.

Dogs romp on the path.
Skaters twirl on the lake.
Under the ice, life
swirls. The yellow chapel
is forever framed by evergreens
and at the end of the pathway
the scene starts over:
The skaters are still
turning, it is still snowing,
turning and snowing.

Moving from solid to scattered
effervescent to evanescent
takes a lifetime.
Everything is nothing
if you look long enough.

Thump

In an old house the noise could be the cat
swatting a Christmas tree ball,
a pile of wobbly presents or stacked books
surrendering to gravity,
the washing machine venting its hatred
of rugs, the refrigerator's harsh cough,
plumbing tying a new knot in itself,
one of the useless chimneys toppling,
a full-length mirror diving off the closet door,
three-legged stool ineptly reglued,
woman or man or dog tumbling down stairs,
some winged thing in attic, basement, bedroom,
a ninety-six-year-old house that sighs and says,
A hundred isn't feasible. I can't.

First Prairie Winter

Nights I lie down in this Kansas
farm town and allow a distant ocean
to swallow my dreams: running on
the boardwalk, Mission Beach, morning fog
burned off in midday sun, the honk and clatter
of humanity, a childhood fear of palm trees,
the stir and noise of family. Lately
I swallow regret the way I once drank love

That brought me here and fell away. I wade
and wallow in winter's dark. Days, the sky looms
large and ineluctable and the land lies quiet, flat
beneath it, accepting everything. It seems that
on the plains people learn early on the rule
of inevitability. I still argue with the clouds.
And each day as I watch the snow deepen by degrees
around the house, I know it might take time for me.

This bed is such a winter, white on white, nothing
near on either side. A chill rides all my surfaces,
mere skin can't shift beyond the reach of Kansas wind.
Sometimes I dream a blizzard that won't stop, that
grows and swells and covers over brittle windows,
settles high. In this dream I run from room to room,
find every window blocked by smothering snow. And
in the lull that follows I go calm at last, settle in

Amid the simple choices. The Pacific ocean
recedes into memory, and in the dark my eyelids lock
beyond old visions. I lie down then, the hard white
windows standing guard, and sleep wrapped in cool sheets
of amnesia while winter's hard fist opens
slowly in the earth, palm warming, long fingers
stirring dormant roots that waken to a new life
easily, easily as I never could by trying.

Five Steps Into A Hard Way

The titmouse comes to the feeder,
the cardinals and the house finch.

There is the mourning dove. She lands
a branch and balances the sway with a lurch
and feather-swell. The ground feeders

industrious find seed, even in snow.
Juncos mostly, and wrens. Small, round birds.

Five steps into a hard way: sparrow
you sit the rooftop. Days pile in white drifts.
The flock thins, scattering at the trouble

of thieving squirrels and larger birds. You stay
an even pitch and eye a sunbleached nest—

too exposed, you wait and gather, wait
and gather yourself, grass-weaver. There's serum
in separation, and a portal. Sleep invisible

below the briar where the dog started
digging. Tuck your beak into a downy shoulder,

one eye bright, one hemisphere
on watch. Tomorrow's circadian rise
will rouse you tomorrow. Tonight, sock in.

Divining the Birds

1
During December's last days,
as mild as May, it rained robins.
They fell from the sky in drops,
clustered in our cedars,
then plopped on the ground.
They paused in mid-migration,
feasting on residual mulberries.
Worms had long since turned
underground. The birds stormed
around us, shitting, starving.
2.
By the river, it was reported
a red-tail hawk attacked a great blue,
its talons snagged the heron's back.
Lingering on late in the season,
the water bird stood meditatively
in the shoals when the hawk,
a stealth bomber, exploded among
its feathers. But in a last arabesque,
the heron swiveled its neck to stab
her enemy's speckled breast.
3.
At dusk, a million blackbirds flow east,
unfurling against a sky, mauve and gold.
No one bird puts a period to this endless
streaming. Tattered wakes of geese
merge into darkness.
Organs steam along the highways.
Bones are spaced along the shoulders.
Soothsayers abound, divining the remains
on earth's altars. None dares predict
how much longer hummingbirds
can negotiate the snow.

Becoming Pioneers

With the furnace out
And snow in the forecast,
They huddle around the wood stove
And journey into 1897.
The surrounding houses dissolve,
Leaving a horizon of white plains.
Wind lurks around timber,
Drawn by lantern light,
Howls echoing into ravines.
Like a gray horse gaunt with starvation,
The bare oak branch nuzzles the window pane,
Begging for sustenance.
How did pioneers stay engaged
On such a night?
Could the same collection of stories
Suffice to stem the tide of loneliness?
Could imagination surge yet again
To create a new even if wholly fabricated tale?
Perhaps contrary to history,
The pioneer's fortitude was not fully tested
By flood, famine, and deprivation.
Only by such a dark night of the soul,
Glancing into the countenance of a spouse
Who has fitted the last puzzle piece
And now stares into your face,
Daring you to be interesting.

Into the Land of Post Rock

"When we build let us think that we build forever. Let it not be for present delight nor present use alone. Let it be such work as our descendants will thank us for; and let us think, as we lay stone on stone, that a time is to come when those stones will be held sacred because our hands have touched them, and that men will say, as they look upon the labor and wrought substance of them, 'See! This our father did for us.'" ~ John Ruskin

It looks as if a drill has marred the sides
otherwise so straight and even
seashells imbedded therein —
rumors of a long-ago sea.
These are the marks of settlers who upon finding
lots of rock, not so much timber
set about to turn the Greenhorn Limestone
into fence posts in Ellsworth, Westfall, Beverly
towns of grandparents' past.
The ingenious pioneers drilled holes,
filled them with water
and waited for the winter freeze to split the rock in two.
Then, slinging the 500-pound posts
under horse-drawn wagons hauled the posts into place.
I've seen photos of the laborers –
wearing overalls, hats pushed back taking their ease at noon
eating lunches made by their German wives or
posed with an uncomfortable pride around the hewn rocks.
My own grandfather
cut posts in the 1920s
when he was newly married
with a family to support.
He went with his father and uncles to cut the rock
working with sledge hammers and wedges,
in the winter, when the carpentry work
and Irv Ekelman's blacksmith shop were slow.
Today, we move the posts with a tractor
and sand-blast on names for decoration.
But customers come with admiration for the pioneers
and want ones with wire embedded still.

With each rock we move, I think,
of the men in the wind-swept winter,
keep moving to stay warm,
to keep food on the table;
and thoughts turn to my grandfather –
taciturn, esteemed, indefatigable.
I look for the marks of his hand.

Kansas Day, January 25

Long winter nights turtles burrow in mud beds
while we drive blotted icy roads. They rest heavy shells
and sleep. Above them, beavers chink domed lodges
and patrol the waterways. Fishing boats hear their slaps.

And in this season of hard weather we gather,
sheltered by timbers and masonry walls.
We repaint ceilings with star animals and hunters.
We remember "Ad astra per aspera" as sun tilts south.

How to Read a Winter Field

Summer's illuminated manuscript is gone.
Nothing green or luxuriant remains.
This field of snow is a severe parchment.
A few autumn grasses penetrate its crust.
Collaborating with the wind, thin stalks
and seed heads scratch back and forth.
This field of snow reveals some basics.
On its plain whiteness, rabbits, mice, coyotes
inscribe histories of frenzied survival.
Throughout the winter they track this field
with skittish penmanship. Their deaths,
blotting it red, are out in the open.
But beneath the snow, voles and weasels
knot into warmth, where no fundamentalist tract
in white and black spells out their dreams.

Icestorm

old elm we named you the Sentinel Tree
high upon the Flint Hills peak
stood winter winds and summers bleak
that did not rip your branches free
there came last night an icy spit
that laid a burden too great to bear
of sculptured glass and crystal glare
and weighted you until you split
the coyote wails of your demise
by sorrow moon and faint starlight
his refuge friend in black of night
no longer there at this sunrise
my young father once sat in view
full of fire and fresh romance
and asked his bride to take a chance
on time and trees that shelter you

Snowstorm

Two of the boys dead before they graduated
high school. One shot by a pumpkin farmer saving
his Halloween crop on a cold October night.
The other killed when his horse threw him.
This boy, more animal than child, came to school
with dirty-faced brothers and sisters
on days when it was too cold in the unheated house
they called home.

The year before, when the snowstorm hit,
the kids slewed their eyes to the schoolhouse windows,
said I needed to let school out before we were snowed in.
I, too focused on the lessons, told them to pay attention
and forget about an early release.

Then the parent showed up at the door and pointed to my VW bug,
almost buried in white. She took the kids, I plowed through
the blizzard-hidden road ten miles to our little house in town.
We didn't leave for days except for my husband's treks
to the grocery store through the snow tunnel in the street,
where he filled a backpack with staples to see us through the siege.

Now, the school sits empty. Country kids ride the school bus to town.
Two boys rode the arc of their lives into the white light of endless night.

The Blanket

Cotton, knit hard, woven tight
and white, some with thin stripes, dark lines
not wide bands of a sailing sky.
Stacked as giant dishtowels near the sink
Here necessities are white, as are waiting sheets
and in dim over-bed light, in a heap near a man's feet,
it is hard to tell sheets from blankets.

At home, a closet full of colors and flowers and stripes,
downy comforters, bolsters, throw pillows and shams.
In the hospice, blankets are layered and covered, required and
not required, bleached. They must absorb, and stuff into rolling carts
easy to wash and steam and whiten, a thousand times over
for the waiting ill, hopeful, the terrified and accepting. A hospital blanket
is no sham. An honest healer, the diffusing filter, a shroud.

If you find yourself curled in a hard vinyl chair one night,
all night, with drowsing cheek to icy fifth-floor window,
you might watch snow fall over a parking lot in the dark
And if the tall steel lamp between spots 62A and 62B
throws light on your father, adrift in his blankets
and every twenty minutes he moans and with large, hairy arms,
arms that hoisted you to see a hippopotamus rise from murky zoo waters,
just in time to see open jaws and a pink hippo tongue, laughing.
He may now fight blankets, rip them from his body
and you may spring from the cold window seat and in haste to throw off
your own blanket you will hit the gray floor, in front of his bed
bound in a white cotton trap, head sideways, seeing under bed bars,
the IV base, the cords and you might think, everything is on wheels.
You will yank yourself up, pat his arm, cover him, breathe,
and the nurses will come to turn dials, and deliver him once again to calm,
to give you two folded blankets. His last warm hours send you back
to the frozen glass grateful now for whatever large white dish towels can give
to blink at parking lights, to hear the snow plow, and wait.

Scene from a Post-Apocalyptic Art Film

Imagine it after everything: it would be the same.
Coarse grass, outcrops of tawny rock. Thickets
of trees matted with dry leaves. The twisted remnants
of a wire fence wreathed with brambles. Maybe
a bird flying in an unforeseeable direction,
and, naturally, the wind, blowing southwest.
Lastly, a small figure walking down the highway
over the eroded paint and cracked asphalt,
singing because there's no one to hear it.

To the Pilgrim Bard, in Gratitude

In honor of my great-great grandfather, the poet Orange Scott Cummins (1846-1928)

I often see you wandering past buffalo wallows, across
black-willow swales, camped under cottonwoods on creek banks,

your mule cart full of bleached bison bones, the air alive
with whippoorwill calls, the ticking whir of rattlesnakes,

wings of wild turkeys rustling in river thickets. I imagine you
writing verse on stripped tree bark, crystallized gypsum,

and flat stones by fitful campfire light. In canyons, on hilltops,
or huddled in your dugout as a Kansas blizzard howls over,

you grip pen and paper with weathered hands under the pale wavering
of a kerosene lamp. In 1871, the Civil War still rattling in your ears,

a photographer's magnesium flare caught that westward slant
in your eye, wide hat-brim circling above long, scout-style curls. Still,

your writing captured more. Poems about ghosts, buffalo herds, Indians,
cowboys, Scots-Irish ancestors, and sodbusters lie buried deep

in your descendants, colorful as the buttes and mesas of the Red Hills
where you settled at last. Fires, floods, family feuds— so much

gets lost. But because we have your words, the wonder holds.
Nothing, not even prairie cyclones, can whisk it all away.

A Kansas Farmwife's Snow Song

Winter weary and all hunkered down, here
with the children and dog this gray day,
how could it seem so far, when you're a mere
quarter section of snowdrifts away.

Broke the ice off the watering trough, dear,
this morning and twice more through the day,
stoked the fire with hedge wood you cut a mere
quarter section of snowdrifts away.

I stared out the window and pondered,
how the snowdrifts don't matter so much.
If it were summer's fields you wandered
I'd still miss your voice and your touch.

At last the end of fence mending is near,
we are about to end this cold day.
Your day's work is done and now you're a mere
quarter section of snowdrifts away.

Reading William Stafford In A Snowstorm

His lines are plowed evenly,
Yet I can seldom predict
Where they will break into drifts.
Here by the bookshelf
Then there by the window
And last, by the blown-open door

Where suddenly I am falling
With the wild driving snow to
Some dark road in Kansas
Which in narrowing its shoulders
To a footpath
Catches me

Shallow like a snow angel, then
Sinking deeper in
The great, cold billows, I find depths
Made for burrowing
Snow caves
Beneath the howling night.

whisper poem

(This poem is to be said in a whisper)

fiercely into the wind
the sky cold and clear
stars glitter, the earth hard
grasses frozen dry
powerful legs pause
nostrils flare
cold dry wind
calm eyes
the ice sings

dot on the horizon

for hours
before it arrived
we could hear
branches of trees rustle uneasily
then ice crystals formed
in perfect math
as stones by the barn
covered themselves in frost
snow and frozen shards
fell in cascades
diamonds and white sapphires
cover the prairie
sharp as knives
lethal

in our home
we wrap our arms
around each other
and wait for eternity to pass

when desire moves

desire moves as a verb, not a noun, consumes like a prairie
   wildfire with gold tongues that lick in flames across pasture
it scorches, lays obsidian carpet, creates life in green blades
   spikes up through cinder and ash, if desire were gemstones
then emeralds-topaz-rubies, it merges victory and surrender
   desire chains, frees, tears down to build up, shifts with the
winds west to east, dangles tart and sugary from the higher
   branch, only ripens on the rarest of trees, desire gathers, has
acquired whole empires, it is the tip of a spire and longing, the
   lover's dance, it is joy, a shining day, it is ours, and hours,
a knotted string of circumstance, desire leaps, it is an intricate
   ballet, it lifts, transports, delivers, blows us back to a time
when life was a field of promise and love was that field on fire

ANNE HAEHL

Changeling: To My Husband

My parents sadly missed
the child the Faery Folk had stolen,
leaving behind their discard,
the oddling, me.
Mother often glanced at the replacement
in vague disappointment, but
my father screamed
at the usurper
of his child's cradle.
Who can imagine then,
who can believe the wonder—
all history turned upside-down--
in your arms
I belonged.

We Read

At the Olpe Chicken House behind glass there's a copy
of Ken Ohm's new book Ducks Across the Moon.
An old woman and her husband cane their way
to the counter, pay with cash, the bills
old and crumbled and green, and ask about the book.
The kid behind the counter, who looks like the town
quarterback, says, "I didn't write it," annoyed,
"Heck, I don't know." And the old couple walks on,
go home, along the way mentioning books they do
know, and love, and read, and then slump in peace, sleep
on their La-Z-Boys, the tv snow, the books
held in their laps, the reading lamps still on.

Fat Tuesday, 2011

The rain falls, falls
Icy and grey in ragged early March.
The sky is not a color but an absence,
Weeping, inconsolable,
Forlorn as music from some dark century.
Rain falls without a thought of stopping,
And underfoot, the yellow brown of wintergrass
Imperceptibly dreams a green beginning.
No crocus or snowdrop has emerged.
The willows by the river are old women
Shivering and naked, no eagles in their branches.
The Kaw runs silty brown, sullen and swollen with inedible fish.
The rain falls, falls
Even the red cars are grey, the dogwalkers
Grim beneath their ponchos
There is a dark, wet light shining everywhere.
The aging bones beneath my flesh cry out
With the knowledge of pain not ending,
Pain raining and falling, cold without end.

A Room of My Own

There's this room inside my head
that no one knows about but me.
You think I'm sitting here with you,
but I'm not, I'm in a corner
of my room where it's dark and quiet
and where no one can find me.
Sometimes I don't come out for days.
That guy you see in his cell or eating breakfast,
playing cards or watching a movie,
that guy you say my name to--
that's just someone who looks like me.
I'm in this room of my own
inside my head, watching you
through two tiny windows.

with the knowing

in memory of my beloved nephew, Sean Patrick Arey, who chose to remove himself from this planet February 28, 2001

two and a half decades before this
godawful month arrived a
darkness gripped his neighborhood:

moms, dads, and kids of all ages search
each white-birched, pined backyard
near-white faces look up and down his street
wide eyes walk the edges of the lake

beneath where he sleeps at night
in his own hiding place
his gray-streaked-black-haired mama
finds him and weeps

yesterday I received word again
we've lost Sean:

my body convulses with the knowing
and I wish to God we could turn back time
to find our precious innocent one asleep
unaware that outside his very bedroom walls
the world searches for him

from the wall-less-ness of wide-sky country
I remember the black-haired baby I cuddled
the dark-eyed little boy I played with
the pimply-faced kid who saved my son
the gray-streaked-black-haired daddy of three

and I weep and know
how you look at a brilliant orange sun
resting at the end of the prairie

and you turn to the east   or to the north
when maybe you shouldn't have turned at all

because you look up a second later
and the sun's gone

Stepping into the Woods

Turn around. The woods have swallowed
you already. The way in is easier
than the way out. Obey these rules:

stay on the path. Do not follow the lights
that flicker on the edge of sight.
Do not eat the bread crumbs,

or listen to the voices, though they echo
through you like the promise of home.
Begin to forget that word: it's only

a place you return to and find
no longer exists. Like a cabin
braced with candy canes, lovely

to see, dangerous to touch.
You'll meet strangers on the way.
Speak to them if you must,

but give them nothing, tell them nothing.
What sharp teeth they have.
Others have come here

before you, but few have left. Curiosity
can consume you. You may think
you see your parents, your lover.

Do not run to them. If you come to a cabin
with legs, walk past it. The skittering
behind you may grow distant in time.

Try not to dream of what may have been.
Distrust what you see. Remember the tale
of the girl who took the stranger's

generosity, how he dragged her

through the streets in a spiked barrel,
or chewed her bones clean. Learn

that trust can kill, and that death
is not the worst thing that can happen
to the young. If you must sleep,

do not dream. The woods enfold
you now, thick as blankets. I tell
you the truth: they are patient

as wolves, hungry as winter.

Driving the Heart

Of this country
on a day too hot for winter
and too beautiful to die, I watch
geese string across our southern sky
while the radio spools news: new car
bombs, polar caps melting, and west,
snow breaks a little our state's long drought.

Once a man told his story: why snakes
lack legs and why you and I
must someday die. But, he said,
until we do, we may sit at the head
of this crowded table.
Many carry that tale
to their hearts, a kind of carrion
they can eat, growing fat
but never full, hungering
for a thing they have forgotten.

Robins come early now, and geese
never leave. Our seasons milder,
we have become their south. Doves
winter in the trees behind our house.
Northward, bears swim
searching lost ice. We drive
a narrow road, leaving heavy tracks.
The clouds ride full to our west.
Let us hope for snow.

Other tales tell of naming, a duty
I have often taken to heart, learning
to call the hawks who ride
our rich winds Red Tail, Cooper's,
Sharp Shinned, as if such things meant
anything. Proud I have been
to own those words.

A cardinal crosses our road,
his red a constant vaunting. The air
waves fill, our leaders' voices loud,
telling us we have everything to fear
and nothing to fret.
Heavy wind blows up from the south,
and the car pulls toward the ditch
not wanting to be steered.

Spring

Begin Again

Magnolia Tree in Kansas

This is the tree that breaks
into blossom too early each March,
killing its flowers. This is the tree
that hums anyway in its pool of fallen
petals, pink as moonlight. Not a bouquet
on a stick. Not a lost mammal in the clearing
although it looks like both with its explosions
of rosy boats – illuminated, red-edged.
Not a human thing but closer to what we might be
than the careful cedar or snakeskin sycamore.
It cries. It opens. It submits. In the pinnacle
of its stem and the pits of its fruitless fruit,
it knows how a song can break the singer.
In the brass of its wind, it sings anyway.
Tree of all breaking. Tree of all upsidedown.
Tree that hurts in its bones and doesn't care.
Tree of the first exhalation
landing and swaying, perfume and death,
all arms and no legs. Tree that never
learns to hold back.

Crow Speaks His Mind

After you have learned all their secrets
And think the way they do . . . they will
fly away and take you with them.
-- Richard Brautigan

Crow ascends from the corner hedge
as if Southwind will lift him above
all creation, then, in his usual way, suspends
himself over my gap gate crossing the two-track
to summer pasture. He's made a habit of hanging
around, watching me open this gate.
I consider Crow from my pickup,
windows down, radio full blast. He hovers
through the weather forecast and a seed corn
commercial, but, at the top of the hour,
with news of the casualty count, he turns
his back, his black robes caught by the wind,
and with a caw like a wail, sails over rimrock
to the bluestem below—where long ago,
he considered my bloody prairie incursion.
Where now, he will pretend I never walked.

The Sod House Green

attached to the wind
is the west wing
of the sod house green
while planting in the spring
I used to say
oh look momma
the sun is rising as the moon is going down
then   look poppa
stop behind the plow
that cloud looks like momma
and like the summer rains
she has gone again
just the growing remains
everything I love
smells like Kansas sod
grown up now
still behind the plow
I kiss the earth
as she rolls over
dark damp and steaming
dinner bell ringing
for the water lost seagulls

Fenceposts

At the southwest corner of the crossing
of two roads in Douglas County, Kansas,
are fields a man staked out with fenceposts
cut from Osage orange, strung with barbed wire.

Did he feel imprisoned by the stark sticks?
Was he sick of doing what they all did?
For some reason, he decided that his fenceposts
should be topped off, crowned with grey rocks.

Was it whimsy or despair that spurred this fancy?
Maybe just a field too full of boulders.
Did the man who would make his mark with fenceposts
fling his ax down, curse the dead wood?

I can see him, straining at his labor
as he harvests, heaves up every capstone,
wires some, as wind howls toward his fenceposts,
thwarts its raging wrath, its lust for emptiness.

Once, my husband, who likes explanations,
said those rocks were set to cover crosscut —
smart thing to do with wooden fenceposts —
if they soak, they rot in spring rain.

Every time I pass, I slow to look again there,
and again try to understand their meaning
for the man known hereabouts for fenceposts
hewn from trunk or limb, stuck in black earth.

Once, I'd visited my father, who lay dying.
All the light he was blazed red behind me,
as I crested the hill beside the fenceposts,
lit the dull rocks, torched them as the sun set.

And I knew the man who put those rocks there
meant them to burn like flames on candles,
unsnuffed by snow, unextinguished by rain,
mutely illuminating, shining through dark night.

Rain

I remember the green pickup,
coming home in the rain.
From the barn to the house
my father carried me piggyback,
beneath his oil-skinned slicker,
below his wet straw hat.

Cocky as a squirrel,
I looked out across
his shoulder at the dark, wet world
and breathed the smell
of damp straw and
manly sweat, felt the closed-in
warmth of blue cotton against
my arms, the certain rhythm
of booted steps in mud, confident
and steady, and I knew
no pelting rain could fall on me.

He might have warned me, "Son,
listen, other rains will come,
pounding shut your eyes
on highways you'll never ask
the name of." (And the miles of rain
I'd know would prove
it true.) But no. Not then.
He gave instead the gift of silence —
bursting like a young oak, fragile
as a bee's wing — as I
rode blue-cotton warm above
my father's booted feet, steadfast
in where we chose
to go and how we meant
to get there.

Lily-flowered Tulips

My hands are covered in dirt.
I dig in dank soil,
dense enough to bend back
the cheap handle of our new-bought
bulb-planting tool. Mosquitoes
blur between my eyes and bangs

and I can't wipe my face from sweat
with these earthen hands. In each
tubed hole, I reach an old spoon
to tap its tip against the brasting bulb.
I am trying to see into the earth

but the dark minions are in my eyes
and the green flopping leaves of hosta
remind me how many things, from
plant to double-headed dog
or gatekeeper waiting for change
are meant to keep me
from seeing or living down into it.

Our world wants up
amongst the bite and sting and sweat.
The dug earth might smell
of wet dog and blackened leaf,
and the tulips might wave to us
each spring coming,

but they're as close as we can get
and not nearly enough: no
merging of our world will ever occur
with that of our still loved
and harder and harder to remember dead.

Equinox

Winter is trying hard to get in a last word, but the calendar
is on my side. So let that gray bastard rant with blustering fists.
I drive home in silence. Grocery sacks spill across the back seat,
frozen vegetables in no danger of thawing in their bags.

Along the street, trees scratch at the sky with skeptical branches--
dates don't make them forgive. They want to be seduced
by longer, warmer days before they'll surrender
in succulent bud.

But daffodils present themselves right now, by the front door.
I bring them inside and bundle them into a vase.
Bright faces watch as I fix supper, elegant guests
join me tonight at my table.

from *earth day suite*

"Your *bad data* caused
these gruesome rebirths! – "

thus the personal gravity
sinks through the woof,

altering time spaces
your footnote, residue,

a missing tile-sliver
from a floor mosaic,

so that someone awakens
with orange on her sole.

I am a woman trapped
in the body of the poem

it makes an epigram of
my epitaph without me.

     *

Thousands of gulls stream
over the fly-overs so
they know it's fall.

The gulls do not fall.
The fly-overs do not fly.

If I could make words into gulls
I would do so. It would not make
me God, but it would solve
many problems.

All my words would go
one way only, up.

The fly-overs are gulled.
The gulls fly over, and out –

Highway 54: Controlled Burn

Eastern Kansas, hills pungent
with controlled burn: my eyes
sting, black clouds rise

into angry evening. All about me,
ribbons of flame unspooled
by grim-faced men with rusty

pickups. Sunglasses
conceal their eyes
as they watch the sky,

the night clear,
free of portentous clouds.
Rain will not come.

And if it did, they would still
burn, unwilling to risk
disaster, fires twisting

from these fallow
fields those newly planted.
Sharp-lined faces know too well

mercy's cost, destroy
what they must to save
the rest. One man turns

his head to watch me pass,
glasses black as his hair
outlined against red flame,

orange sky. He nods,
I nod, accelerate
toward home, towards

whatever still remains.

Abject Impermanence in Kansas

for Jamie D'Agostino

It wasn't so long ago
Then it was longer than we thought.
Really it was a step or two beyond thinking.
The edge is out there somewhere.
The photograph I'm holding proves it.
Here's another friend who has fallen into a frame
And nowhere else.
In the closet, there's a shoebox holding a wallet-sized
Grand Canyon and the largest ball of string in Kansas.
Immutability was not a dream than it was.
Now we have nothing and don't care either.
Ontologically rich, metaphysically poor,
The non-substance of any living.
Some people die with their boots on, not making it
out of the trenches or even a few feet farther.
Our boots are only muddy.
Anyone can track us down.
We reinvent desertion and call it flight
only to be arrested and fall too easily from the sky.
Be careful which way you point that gun.
We want to see your license for extinction.
Twigs snap, snap again.
Now we're running fast.
The arrhythmia of rumors causes us to stop
And catch a breath.
The canary long ago dead in the deep tunnels
Of our visions. No answer was ever forthcoming.
When the stage was finally reached
No one arrived to play the part.
The horizon pulled back. Curtains in flames.
Cowboys gasp in dust behind cattle
Headed for Abilene.
The Flint Hills napped into gravel.
Who will be next to wake?

Tornado Symptoms

As you step outdoors you'll enter a hot barn
with a moist haystack inside.
The cardinals will dart like embers, pierce
pierce your nerves with their bent sabres.
You'll be intimate with traffic for miles around.
But if you look up where the twigs
all stiffly point, you'll see silent
pandemonium, ugly rumors,
vagrant clouds loitering at loose ends.
It's a schizophrenic air.

By supper the sky will be uprooted,
a garden hopelessly gone to seed.
Gray broccoli will float by disconnected
from the ground, fat sooty toadstools,
a species you've never seen before,
will sprout beside swollen fungi
and other gray growths, strange weeds trailing
their severed roots, flowers the color
of bad bruises just opening into blossom,
slowly moving areas of combustion.
Even cauliflower as it rolls past
will be misshapen
before the forest comes.

Microburst

You were just awake when the windows
jumped in and out of themselves.
It was an insurrection you felt
in your feet as the tree branches
leaned toward the house, frantically scratching
"let me in." The cat
had long since sheltered
behind the refrigerator when
the first thunderous reports began
twitching the foundation,
shivering crossbeams, worrying
the studs. The electricity
felt like betrayal, the shuddering wind
a burgeoning anger. By the time the cat
was back to wander the kitchen
all those aches coursed toward
sunken intersections, you were
once more too tired to be happy,
too tired
to check for damage.

Disaster (or Bum Rap)

She spent her adult days
worrying about the inevitable:
earthquakes in L.A.,
stacking escape clothes
by her bedside in case
she had to make a run for it
in the middle of a dream,
or pursued by New York thugs
out to steal her innocence...
and variations on that theme.

In Mid-America where she
rejoiced from lack of stress,
her mind and limbs
relaxed enough to avoid
the muscle cramps she suffered
in L.A. and NYC. She forgot
about the bedside clothes
double locks, and being alert
and ready to avert disaster.

And so she was taken by
complete surprise when
in the middle of a placid dream,
a tornado lit down on the roof
of her house and whisked away
all her cares, leaving her
naked and alone in a field
where her house had stood,
in full view of the moon
shining overhead and
on both coasts simultaneously.

ISRAEL WASSERSTEIN

A Kansas Native Discusses Natural Disasters

Raised in California, you freeze with each storm warning,
listen for the locomotive roar,
imagine the funnel cloud descending
dark against greenblack dusk.
Strange, I thought. You know
the earth can swallow cars, buildings,
that land can collapse to sea,
that the next Big One is inevitable.
Yet a twister might pass blocks away
and leave us unaware until sirens woke us.
But now I know: you are a child of the land.
Amidst its tremors you brace under doorframes
without fear. I was raised by sky,
its furies as much as its calms.
When the evening chills with the hammer of hail,
the air takes me breathless, tense, home.

Prairie Idyll

Hail-stripped cottonwoods
weep like battered wives;
yesterday's wheat fields molder
in galvanized tombs.

It's been this way before:
the patriarchal sun turning
his gray side out like a banker
locking his door.

Main streets lie fallow
as desert bones. Tumbleweeds
dance on doorsteps.
Logo caps commiserate
round gun-racked pickup trucks
while only the crow's cry

mocks the stillness. And I—
turning a shoulder to the dark wind—
pilgrimage past the boarded school,
slip the wrought-iron portal's latch,
drop to one knee and lay a peony
on my mother's grave.

Unhindered

Barred owl sings her low thrum
under chill spring moon

above gutter-rimmed gables and pin oaks,
mid-continent, midnight, mid-dream.

She sends each pulse
to throb in my middle-ear--

feather drawn across
this nerve,

this pulse-point, brace
of wrists, braced--

Barred owl eye wisens, wine-dark, aglow--
small planet in its orbit--

Pure motion, dropping through the branches from her heaven--

No entanglement is love.

There! There!

First the early-morning
cup of coffee to my lips
while herons fly over
on their way to the Kaw
from the Haskell Bottoms,
wetlands only fourteen blocks
south of my fenced yard.
In silence, they glide above us.
Starlings whirring, hunker down
as if they saw hawks or hot air balloons.
So, picking up my brush to paint –
to make the circle of my day come
true - I think how pleasant is the town
that embraces these beautiful creatures.
Darkness comes again, shadows filling inside
Fences. Flowers lose colors as light puts itself to bed.
Once again the prayer of holding my evening glass.
Water tonight. Tomorrow some of the new wine.
Heat leaves the day and tomorrow
winter will want our attention.
But sometimes in the dark, just
as the end seems imminent,
geese sew the crest of the wind.
Sparks of dying light
reflect in the water.
We see it.
There!
There!

Senses

a sparrow sings outside the glass
Ann senses a coming question
his finger tracks down her forearm
cotton sheets crisp like sandpaper
fresh laid carpet now springs upward
then of course there is the sweet taste
of cold peaches sublime peaches
the musty brick smell of street rain
small girls whispering a secret
warm of sun and cool of shadow
cry for milk baby cry for milk
mystery of thunder without
the scalpel stab wound of lightning
how does he dare express his hope
how does he ask her quiet face
my love do the blind dream in feel

Beside a Country Road

She had dug her den wisely
where the turn of a driver's
gaze would have to slot into
a second's synchronicity
or the grass and the rock would
keep her secret, as she knew.
I had slipped through the crack
in a moment's privilege and kept
her secret. Such confidence is
salvation in a world burning
with our hungers. – You out there
in your den, let me hold you close
in the cool darkness where your
tongue laves the little ones to life.

Ebenfeld Churchyard

A shovelful of dirt strikes the casket.
He played golf one afternoon in May
and the next day, was no longer.

It's raining here on the prairie
behind the country church he loved.
How does my gentle cousin
not wake up in the morning?

Was it fifty years ago, when
tiring of coloring books,
we played under grandma's table
wondering which one of us
she loved the most?

Was it only fifty years ago,
when dashing across a farmyard
I stumbled, splitting my knee open,
and he felt guilty because
he won the race?

It's raining here on the prairie
behind the country church he loved.
The tent over the gravesite
is of no use to me.

Memorial Day on the Prairie

Each year we plod through spring rain
or dry heat, step with care around new-broken
graves and fresh sod, nod to marbled pride,
generations with the same names as those

still alive back in town. We carefully poke
plastic roses into the ground and whisper
the ritual words. Red for the sister:
"It was her favorite color." She died

when a drunk in a pickup smashed her red car.
Yellow for the father: "He was so cheerful."
Except when his last years robbed him
of breath and speech. White for the stillborn

child, who wore the cord around his neck.
Sleeping in sacrificed wheat fields, these
are our loved ones: decades of harvested crops,
bread turned to stone, alone and blind

to these witnesses, scarved heads bowed.
Out here on the prairie, the wind never stops.

Conversations with my Mother's Picture

You and Dad were entirely happy here—
you in purple miniskirt, white vest and tights
(you always wore what was already too young
for me), Dad in purple striped pants,
a Kansas State newsboy's cap
made for a bigger man's head.
You both held Wildcat flags and megaphones
to cheer the football team who,
like the rest of the college, despised you
middle-aged townies, arranging for their penicillin
and pregnancy tests and selling them
cameras and stereos at deep discount.
But you were happy
in this picture, before they found
oat-cells in your lungs.
After the verdict, he took you to Disneyland,
this man who married you and your five children
when I was fifteen. He took you cross-country
to visit your family, unseen
since your messy divorce.
He took you to St. Louis
and Six Flags Over Texas and to Topeka
for radiation treatments.
I don't think he ever believed
you could die. Now he's going
the same way. And none of us
live in that Wildcat town with the man
who earned his "Dad" the hard way
from suspicious kids and nursed
your last days. For me, this new dying
brings back yours, leaving me only this image
of you both cheering for lucky winners.

The Woman Doing Cartwheels in the Living Room

She is the woman doing cartwheels in the living room. Her hands press into carpet, collect pebbles and crumbs. Her legs pinwheel the air. The windows clatter and expand, tissue paper in the wind or mirrors crowding around her, waiting to see her fall.

When she was young, she tore lettuce rather than cut it. She said if you used a knife it would bruise too soon. That was a long time before, and she was a blonde then. All the men saw her hips swish when she walked by.

She likes the way the walls swirl before her, the lining in the wood panels their own veins, dizzied and open, draining onto the baseboards, then the floor, where she focuses her eyes when she spins.

The woman doing cartwheels in the living room sees faces at night. They are smudged with dirt and mouth words she cannot hear. The faces remind her of the children she never wanted to have, the eyes she finds in her dreams, the small hands pulling at her shirt sleeves. She covers her head with a blanket.

She thinks of the black-lit rooms, the empty bed down the hall. Her hands ache. Her feet are scratched and scarred from slipping on tile. Her mind is a snowy highway with dull lights. She cannot remember how to stop skidding.

She is the woman doing cartwheels in the living room. Her jean shorts are frayed at the edges. Her shirt falls, exposing fire scars on her belly from pregnancy. She tucks in her shirt and it comes undone, and she cannot hide it from the world.

Columbarian Garden

Cold sun brings this mourning season to an end—
one year since my mother's death. Last winter thaw
my brother shoveled clay-dirt, she called it gumbo,
over what the crematorium sent back. Not her,

but fine, powedery substance, lightened, all else
rendered into invisible elements. That handful
from the pouch, un-boxed, was tucked into plotted soil,
the churchyard columbarium, a brass plaque the last

permanence, and the brick retaining wall.
Now my mother is a garden—day lilies and chrysanthemums
feeding from that slight, dampened, decomposing ash.
Her voice stilled. One ruddy robin in the grass, dipping.

Bestiary: Henbit (Lamium Amplexicaule)

Many are there over mid-earth,
the lowly henbit. Lamented
as weed. Nicknamed "giraffe-
head" for its haughty, mottled,
orchid-flower and tuft of fuchsia
fuzz. Lauded as wildflower. Its ruffled
leaf an Elizabethan ruche
around the square empurpled stem.
When in April it comes again,
spring's wakening it leads.
Not much alone, but abloom
across a furrowed field it spreads
a gaudy undulating stain
and shouts the end of winter's gloom.
So too, do we, united and in flower,
take back our country and our power.

Restored Victorian

I bought a bucket of Morning-Dew
and painted windows open.
Toasted-Pine-nuts that splattered the floor
were patiently scrapped with razor and rags
until the oak grain shone.
Evocative-Sunlight in multiple layers
hid bruise marks on the walls.
Two blankets of Ivory-Coast
covered tenderly mended kicked in doors.
Frosted-Hawthorn soothe with brush strokes
graffiti from drunken frat-boy parties.
The painted Victorian stood,
as it had for a hundred years and more,
patiently waiting for its wounds to heal.
Next morning I brought a gallon
of Good-As-New and sealed
the front porch done.

Site Fidelity

We survey the grass blades for seeds, for a place
as my arm wraps around you like thicket
because I fear I'll lose you through the sumac and tallgrass
tipsy from the wine of bitter Kansas grapes

while my left hand snags your cocklebur hair
the same way men treat the prairie, you say,
the way men pull at its covers until bare,

so we take turns examining the ground for surface scars,
for what was planted, as if our own bodies—the mark
down my back, the one you have but can't show, and the one
on your hip that the sun sets shadows upon—
as darkness is catching up with the dark that exists,

and you admit you were afraid to come out here
because of coyotes, the animals wild at night,
after I admit I am afraid of night itself,
how it washes the red sky with indigo, with shadows
widening on our faces, on my open arms of hillsides,

and as you trace the backwards question mark
of the lion that only protects the night sky in spring,
you whisper how we are the cardinals
we hear, returning home,

as you close your eyes first, as we slip
into the landscape our lips make
with its tinge of cedar from prairie fires,
the taste of restarting,

of those crimson feathers rising
in rows of birds that migrate back
free, restless, and blazing—

The Three Times in my Life when I've Read William Stafford's *Key of C - An Interlude for Marvin*

We were on the road between our homes
speaking only of each other, instances and secrets.
You read to me on the way,
your voice elliptical in turns
and surroundings of stanzas and statements.
I saw the poem first through your voice:
all of them telling their futures,
their secrets to come to hold them fast to time.
I had to cry for their fates.
It seemed like our moment was in theirs,
the uncertainty of our timelines placed to sight.

She was born sometime later.
I had forgotten the poem as time travelled us
toward embraces of three.
I stumbled upon it and was stopped like a short breath.
I saw the poem through the both of you,
close by on the bed, in your light and sighing
moment of arms and nothing but that.
I had to cry for you and them
in the gathered instant of gathered fortune,
knowing how tightly you would always hold her.

The sun shined setting through
the windshield of the locomotive.
The air-conditioning and my shaded safety-glasses glinted it away.
I found the book of poems in my bag and read the poem again.
I was sure of my emotions in my surroundings of reflecting steel,
ballast black from loose oil and a co-worker stranger beside me.
But still, behind my glasses I had to cry for the poem.
The gentle giving. The gentle giving.
I put the book away and turned from the stranger,
bent to reach for a bottle of water from the ice bucket,
not offering one to him.
The poem swirled into me as cold water.

Stubble and Sleeping

Stubble and sleeping on sod that is softened
by the freeze and thaw of the soil.
Green blades and mixed grasses are paths for the ants
And the thatch for the birds building nests
Rosette of the mullein I open to find
A sensuous insect within its soft cupped leaves.
It is spring and I plant my thoughts on paper in a chair
And dream of tornadoes full of flowers.

Tornado Drill

I wore my backpack backwards,
so with cleaving textbook corners
and the weight of bologna and a fruit cup,
I was pregnant fleeing the great drone

of the tornado drill tornado.
I lost a shoe in the gleaming hall
and shy Kelly, who played the trombone in music,
rescued it for me, pinching the ribbon.

Safely shepherded into the capsule gymnasium,
we hugged our wooden knees and balloon hearts,
tucked our crystalline brains down
at the place in our bodies where the halves
of future babies stirred and sighed.

The fake tornado felt like my father
when his veins wormed plumper
and his words became spit.
I was banished to my room.
I stood, braced my aching
book weight, and went.

The Seventh Year

That's how it started --
driving across Kansas on a wave of the blues,
poems working their way to the surface
bearing messages of stone and fern,
soul and bone and dirt.
The seventh year is the one when
everything changes -- you've seen it coming
like a tornado on the horizon.
The sky turns black and yellow and green,
you run for the storm cellar
and play gin rummy on a rickety card table
next to the canned goods,
then sleep piled on the floor like puppies.
When birds carol the new day,
the sky like a basket of clean cotton towels,
nothing has changed but
everything is new.

You Look Beautiful

The husband says, "You look beautiful."
Not hearing, the wife says,
"Have you seen my glasses?"
"I said, you look beautiful."
"Well, let's find my glasses
And we'll see."

How to Skype

Take the basic craving to watch your beloved in motion --
emptying his pockets onto the bookshelf,
approaching with telltale gait,
thumbing his beard thoughtfully --
and crumple it in your hands
like a troublesome poem.

Listen to distant wind chimes and barking dogs, watch
curtains fluttering on ever-lovely West Coast mornings
from your Midwest thunderstorm afternoon.

Make like your heart is a rusted bolt,
and pry at it with pliers, with numbed fingers.
Fumble with scissors and kitchen knives
until under the grime, bright silver scrapes
wear the edges away.
Until even the right wrench
could never loose it.

Centering the House

All night Kansas
the lungs of the continent
takes a sip of the galaxy

swirling stars and barbed wire
sofabeds and willows
books and doors banging open

signs disappear whole towns
ditch themselves in the countryside
I stir the coffee to center the house

the place our mothers and fathers
and theirs and theirs passed through
their aprons strung on telephone wires

this tunnel of wind this trial
makes trees throw back their heads
and the hair along our arms stand up

we're nothing but breath on its way through the woods

Sweet Storm

I sleep under a tin roof.
When it rains we are dancing,
almost a flamenco, but more scattered.
Our petite Rain Deity presents a tiny
machine gun that soothes our ears.
I bound from the arms
of my grandmother's bed
and praise what Gods there be
for the night I have spent
half with you and half alone.
The grey skies are not like a battleship,
more resplendent as the nuthatch calls,
more vibrant as my heart and head tangle
with a rush that is only mine.
This is no day to force the forsythia.
It will grow in its time,
a time for which I cannot wait

Cow Creek

When I went out, Cow Creek let me in.
The creek hid me. The creek taught
me words and to worship its thrust.

The willow would announce spring.
Catkins called me into the wet.

April was water spilling into the yard,
creeping up, turning my rivulet torrent.

When ejected indoors by wind and rain,
the creek still whispered in a vestigial voice
words like home that bathed me in shelter.

Time

God gave the white man clocks,
            the Ghanaians time.
                        —Ghanaian saying

Was it the bluejays woke me
with their cawing and shrieking—or
was it the foxes barking at an owl?
Suddenly, loudly, I am awake,
bolt upright in bed. My husband,
snoring lightly beside me, doesn't move
or turn as I go from room to room
shutting doors and drapes against intrusion,
trees still black against the paling grass,
descending sky. No doors out there
in the real world. On my own, I
wouldn't know the twilight from
the dawn—could work or sleep around
the clock. Only time would tell
the difference—its tiny hands
inching their way across my life.

Begin Again

Go back and do it again,
my father told me.
And I would lift up my hoe,
dragging my feet through
the dusty rows
of beans and a few weeds
to start the first row
I started an hour ago.
Lifting the hoe for the first pull,
dragging dirt around the plant,
kachunk – flicking out a weed.
The rhythm of pulling in,
the dance of flicking out.
Beginning from the right,
I would fall into the dream

See the hills: watch the horses
beginning from the right come in
and make a straight line
tied to the leather rope
strung between two trees.
The women walk behind,
carrying bundles and babies.
The men stand and wait, watching carefully
and the children run among each other like little goats.
The soft eyes of the young women watch
the unmarried boys
begin again.

Mother said this needs more work.
Go back and do it again.
And I would put each dish
back into the pan,
filled again,
scrubbing each dish.
The rhythm of circling in,
the dance of circling out.
Beginning from the left,
I would fall into the dream.

See the road: watch the cars
beginning from the left come in
and make a circle,
headlights pointed inward
against the coming dark.
Women carry pans and dishes
to the tablecloths spread in the field.
The men carry babies, drums and rattles.
The children who can, run
against each other like little bulls.
The soft eyes of the young women watch
the unmarried boys
and begin again.

My father's garden grows enough
for the critters, neighbors and for our family.
He said, if it doesn't come up,
go back and plant again.
And I would find the place
where crow had danced,
where mole worked his blankness, and
the bug children had eaten
more than their share.
The rhythm of planting again,
the singing in empty places.
Beginning from the center,
I would fall into the dream

See the storm: watch the water
beginning from the center, come in
and fill the wetlands,
rush the ditches.
Bloom the flowers.
The birds fly through us,
standing on the walkways.

The water changes colors
as we pass through,
while the children expand like popcorn
with the beauty.
And the questions find answers.
Living we go back.
Learning, we come forward.
Our return is our prayer.
We began again.

Summer

Begin Again

I, in Fellowship

after Whitman

White tail converge in morning dew
    conferencing over some farmer's new beans in casual dozens.
Mourning doves line barbed-wire fences and power lines,
    nattering above walk-in hunting fields marked with blaze orange ribbons.

Armadillos shoot through brush that clumps up ditches,
    steps ahead of mowers carving space for autumnal flash floods.
A bobcat hunches along the hedge-row, on the trail of breakfast,
    unconcerned with the coffee-klatch of nettles chattering in her fur.

An opossum rattles along the road, oversized teeth clacking at anything
    edible, from the three-days dead to truffle-shaped rocks.
Turkey vultures hold congress around a raccoon. They're stuck in filibuster:
    It's not dead. It's the wind. Can we eat it? Look for possum. Go up the road.

A blue heron sticks his nose up at the thick waters of his strip-mined pond,
    lifts a leg, flaps a wing, but eats the sun perch anyway.
An alligator gar grins like a fancy television wrestler, swishes
    through eddies into the river, looking for small fry.

Grass—green, brown, yellow, and orange—plays percussion for the wind.
Trees, in tuxedoes of moss, dance the minuet of creaky bark.
Corn twitters in its rows, twisting its gossip until it sounds like popping.

I brush my hair from my face. The wind pushes my clothes. Rain licks my feet.
The sun tastes my flesh. I resonate Kansas.

The Night We Heard the Whippoorwill

The night we heard the whippoorwill,
we sat on rocks in Constant Park,
our hair mussed from the wind.
The florets of love-lies bleeding
held red in spite of the darkness.
We watched Cassiopeia and Orion
slow-dance to moon music.

Blowing the sure laws of physics,
clouds rolled behind the moon.
You slugged me and spoke of horses,
horseflies, horse-sense, how they
converge in the plausible world.
Fireflies looped above the grass.
Fog ghosted through the trees.

The night we heard the whippoorwill
was not the last night of our lives.
That night came in winter,
when the nightjar's song was silent,
and the dirge of dead oaks
drove us to the high loess
cliffs above the river.

Profession

for the teachers

Has summer ever not wound to school,
wounding me with its insistent buzz and chirp:
work, work, work; done and gone, done and gone.

I try to freeze the days with compressors and sleep,
keep the nights as late as I can, blinking dots and books.
A few tasks, the mechanic's, the stylist's, the party, and the jaunt.

When the moon blooms full and bright as marigolds
and the naked ladies pop up pink and plain as ever
while the marsh mallows wave over small rooftops,

and the cicadas are stunned and dragged down
into burrows to live twice their lives
as food for some other species' young,

we wake again and go, we teachers, we book-holders,
we paralyzed buzzers, our hair trimmed and our clothes new,
we go unarmed into their burrows, bringing our lives along.

Hunting for Arrowheads

I am trying to learn a language,
but I don't now what it is,
a common practical type
like charades
when by miming
I am elated that you have guessed
an approximation
of what I really want to say
like in the Sahara that time when
a boy herder and I were
discussing the existence
of arrowheads in the sand
as there are on the Kansas prairie
giddy to have finally found
something recognizable
on the dusty path of our conversation
we planned to look for them on
Wednesday
only now it is
Thursday
some twenty years later
and we still haven't gone
but that could be inconsistency
in how we each view time
it is more foreign in our bedroom
where we have communicated children
even you
appear clearly puzzled
by some lack
a point, maybe
I will find one
if I'm lucky

Chicken Egg Grenades

As a boy, I remember the belt
Two inches wide, brown leather
Folded and snapped to pop
Before the licking

I suppose I deserved the
Lash, a voice of discontent
At the end of a summer's day
The battle bathed the backyard

A German soldier here
A Japanese brigade there
They needed the pin pull
And boom to guard home
And save my mid-state family

The chickens did
Not miss the two
Hundred; they would
Never see the hatch

Not Yet Flying

The velvet bump
of tadpoles against my
palm, hundreds
of fat, black bodies
wiggling in the galvanized
tub, bodies my brother
planned to make bait or money.
My sister and I plotted
to release them,
half-legged and stubby tailed.
When we picked up the tub
between us, they sloshed
and plopped on the patio
like ripe cherries.

My brother sent
the bait man's three dollars
away with a comic book
coupon and we teased him
when the thick envelope
arrived marked Joe Weider,
Trainer of Champions.
All that summer my brother
left his t-shirt on
to hide his belly.

My son's sharp shoulder
blades stick out like wings.
We go to find tadpoles.
I want to show him how
their comet shapes sprout
legs and front arms and
stand-up eyeballs.
We kneel beside the sandpit,
barely a ripple in the water,
only carp, and a throaty
vibration from a clutch
of frogs.

A Hayloft Belongs to Children

The mice, given gray color by their God
Slide unseen under scythed summer hay
Loose in the loft, two inches of tan straw
Dross from collected bales stored above

They steal the feed from two draft horses
Below that cool their coats from the middle
Of summer heat after they plowed their
Existence from the world of pre-seeded fields

They hide, when children, cousins who cling
To a smooth rope that hangs from an old
Hand-carved block and tackle, tarzan east then
West onto the mown stacks of fodder

Their constant motion under the ship keel of
Trusses create tables for tea, stadium seats to
Watch winning teams, and Tibetan mountains
To climb as the light moves to end the day

Creek Play

If you look closely,
small, freckled limbs,
not yet diagnosed with MS,
make their way boldly
up a dusty hill once
mountainous in size.
A creek, both deep and dry,
drew us in season after season
as our bodies changed
and dreams grew larger
than the sky.
Hiding, playing
cowboys and Indians,
each passing car
a threat from near and far.
Years later, shared dates and
hope for future plans
left less time and attention
to barren, rugged beauty
of the land.
To climb those hills,
fill my nose with the dusty smell
of Kansas, sneezing out
the ability to be young again.
We searched for fossils,
dinosaur teeth and arrowheads,
found rattlesnakes and cow skulls.
I became a mother and a writer.
You manufactured crack -
just think about that.
If we went back and did it again,
would the sunset still inspire,
would our desire to escape
have changed?
Would my body, spasming in pain,
be made whole again?
Would you still be imprisoned,
feeling the brutal Kansas winter
from within a castle prison
on the prairie?

Western Meadowlark

for Ana

Through the open car window
seven needles in a haystack
BoPEEP-doodle-our-PEOple!
snatched by ear out of the moving
prairie, like you
already fading, passed, gone.
BoPEEP-doodle-our-PEOple!
If I could find it, it would be
points of sunlight glancing
off a brooch so near shades
of gold in these moving
grasses I could scarcely distinguish
it from the grasses. Like you
it is always gone.

BoPEEP-doodle-our-PEOple!
The bird pulled it off like a string
of catches on this flying
trapeze which keeps swinging
back. If birds' songs simply mean
I'm here! I'm here!
then why a song so baroque?
How many notes did it have?
Which notes were extra?

In the Beatles' "Blackbird"
you again hear a meadowlark, its song
canned as the slow-motion replay
of a pass-reception on TV:
Love studied into pornography,
Bo-PEEP-diddk-diddk-her-PEEP-hole!
The bird falls off a see-saw,

hesitates, picks itself
back up on the rising board,
completes its song.
It does it again.

I prefer the song that eludes me,
this one which we are passing,
banjo music picked out
through wind and distance
already falling behind

gone and not gone.

Dreams and Consequences

As if someone whispers my name
I awake. In darkness the scent
of swathed hay drifts through open windows.
A bird has yet to herald dawn. Even so,
the transient sweet air pulls me
out of night. Sense and thought collide.

In the small nursing home down the road
Mother too most likely lies awake.
Her windows are shut, sounds and smells
trapped inside. Sleep has escaped her
for days, but not dreams. They crook
their fingers, dare her to follow.

If I knew someone with money and a car,
she muttered yesterday, her face set hard,
I'd get the hell out of here, as if
it were the Dirty Thirties and she,
stuck in dusty old Kansas. I picture
a lit cigarette sitting beside her
in a heavy glass ashtray, her eyes
squinting through a coil of smoke.

The fragrance of raked alfalfa
and something more, something dark
and fresh, circles me. It belongs to
rope swings, bicycles, clothes on the line,
Mother handing me a laundry basket
before she turns back to frying chicken.
It belongs to the pop-pop of the old
John Deere 70, to young hired men,
to Dad showing how to work a clutch.

As windows glimmer like ghosts
I stay where I am, knowing the day
will break like any other. The carrier
will deliver the paper, the first
bird will soon call out, and then
I will rise, not minding too much
this early start. It is, after all, summer
and fledglings sing for the first time
and sail from tree to tree, determined
to answer to instinct, to fly on their own.

MICHAEL L. JOHNSON

Laura Gilpin, *The Prairie*

Platinum expanse: open, endless plain
dotted with forbs but ironing-board flat.
Wisps of clouds, windswept, reach across wide sky.
Down in the left corner a woman stands
posed, softly vertical in that stretched space,
face toward the sun, white skirts billowing
silently. She stares into nowhere, hand
cupped to her ear.

Flint Hills Patriarch

The old elm suckled from this seep before
cattle drank from the Neosho, when
bison angled trails from water to water
and Kansa were people of the land.

It wrestled Southwind,
carried its omnipresent weight,
bowed in submission yet took strength
from it. Standing alone in the tall grass

like a tilted vase, it reaches
for those who belonged, points
at those who lost faith and inquires
of those who pass by.

A Skulk of Foxes

Like the cherm or charm of finches, so the skulk of foxes
confounds the twilight. Step-sidling, their auburn pelts shift
into shadows. Cat-like, they stalk mice. Shanks turn black.
Slit eyes catch last yellow sunlight and hold it steady.
They den down the block, under the neighbor's tool shed.

Tomorrow they might turn into fancy stoles or tricksters.
They might turn into ragged coyotes and grin at gardeners.
They could be a skulk of thieves, crouched. Or malingerers.
Under mulberry shrubs they sense human presence. Pause.
Flicker in peripheral vision, softly scatter. But never vacate.

Summer Storm Among The Strip Pits

I have parked on a dump that overlooks
the water. Kingfishers slap surface,
dip and cut wide figure eights, lifting

like flapping hands into the sky.
Rain comes, peppering the surface
like thousands of winged insects, tapping

light fingers against the roof of my van.
Curtains blow. From the tops of poplars
I hear the wind moan, turning the alkali

over upon itself, the clay mixing
with gray shale, trickling
down from the tailings. The small soil

that runs between roots of a willow
clouds the vacant water
and spreads like the spawn of fish.

I Was Living My Life

Last week, my dear Deborah encountered a deer
I didn't know anything about it
I was living my life
Weeding the sweet potatoes
Watching movies
Enjoying a swim at Toronto State Lake
and meanwhile, my dear Deborah crashed on the road.

Yesterday, my friend, Mark,
died after a routine surgery on his knee.
I didn't know anything about it
I was living my life
Sharing the bounty of our peach tree
Writing policies for the Behavioral Sciences Regulatory Board
Collecting money for the New Boston Food Coop
and meanwhile, my friend Mark passed on from a post-op blood clot.

Today, I am living my life
Digging up turnips
Painting the trim at the cabin
Meditating with the Buddhists
I wonder what else is going on?

We Discuss the Geomorphology of Life

It's called saltation, I said,
when grains of sand are picked up by the wind
and blown along, dislodging other grains,
building dunes the size of houses.
The wind is blowing the seconds of our lives away
just like that, saltating seconds into minutes and hours and days.

No, she countered,
it's like surface waves on the ocean,
the wind pushing and shoving and the waves building
until they crash on shore, pounding
and wearing down everything in their path;
it's like that, we float from crest to trough,
day to night, spring to fall,
the horizon bobbing in and out of view
the cliffs drawing nearer with each rise, each fall.

You're both wrong, you said,
it's like a flash flood in the desert,
rain drops turning soil to mud, mud floating away in rivulets,
in spates, in torrents;
we are tumbling end over end
with water in our eyes and ears and mouths and lungs
never seeing exactly where we are heading,
but always accelerating down the canyon of time,
slowing only as we approach the wide, flat valley floor,
bereft of breath,
covered with silt,
estuarine in our end,
one with the earth in our completion

Summer in Kansas

Summer in Kansas is why,
despite the legislature,
despite the Board of Education,
and the specter of God in politics,
there is space for the atheist.

Argument by design; the perfect
balance of day and night, the fine
cocktail of oxygen and carbon dioxide,
the unaided perfection of the eye—
it all falls apart in August

when the sun, the moist smothering
atmosphere, and the burning winds
all stand forth against the lives
of every worshiper and every
blasphemer to show us this world

was not made for us, and we
are not so well made for this world,
and the only defense against this creation
is a tiny air conditioner of
decidedly un-divine design.

Figurative North Topeka

for Ben Lerner

Seasonal graffiti crawls
up the overpass like ivy —
abstract names on concrete stanchions.
To the south, symbolic walls:
NO OUTLET signs along the levee,
idle river, idle tracks,
bypass, bluffside and the backs
of Potwin's late-Victorian mansions,
flush like book spines on that shelf.
Drunk on your late-Victorian porch
you promised me that if elected
you'd have the river redirected
down Fourth Street, to make Potwin search
North Topeka for itself.

I told you to retire *Ad Astra*
Per Aspera and put *For God's*
Sake Take Cover on the state
          seal and flag — the license plate
at least, since we collect disaster
and death like they were classic rods:
'51 Flood; '66 Tornado.
Even the foot-lit Statehouse mural
has a sword-bearing Coronado,
a Beecher's Bible-bearing Brown
and a tornado bearing down
on its defenseless mock-pastoral,
The Past. The present was still wet
when the embarrassed legislature
resolved that it would never let
John Steuart Curry paint the future.
He never did, although Topekans
would learn to let bygones be icons.

*   *   *

On Thursday, July 12, the rain
relented and the water rose,
darkened and stank more. The stain
is just shy of the second story
in what used to be Fernstrom Shoes.
That entire inventory
spent five nights underwater, gaping
like mussels on the riverbed.
Fernstrom spent the summer scraping
gobs of septic-smelling mud
out of eleven thousand toes.

On Friday the 13th, the Kaw
crested at thirty-seven feet.
They thought it might have cut a new
channel down Kansas Avenue.
One *Capital* reporter saw
a kid reach up from his canoe
and slap the stoplight at Gordon Street.

Porubsky's never did reclaim
its lunchtime clientele; the torrents
sent the Sardou Bridge to Lawrence
and there was no more Oakland traffic.
Business hasn't been the same
for fifty years now. Fifty-two.
Ad astra per aspera: through
the general to the specific.
        You do what you want to do
but I'm not using North Topeka
in conversation anymore
because there is no north to speak of;
there's only mud and metaphor.

Kansas Freaks

Once in awhile a touch like the above.
–Joseph Cornell

If I have to remember something about 1966, let it be Frank Zappa and the
      Mothers of Invention,
their first record release, Freak Out. It was Christmas vacation and looking for
      something to set me apart
from the dull Midwest, I bought the album for its psychedelic neon cover before
      I'd heard the word psychedelic.
My favorite line, sung longingly, "With hair growing out every hole in me," as if
      their one wild moment
had already fallen to the barbershop floor. Perhaps they were right, thirty years
      later, the band broken-up,
Frank dead of prostate cancer, my turntable up in a puff of smoke, signaling the
      century's end,
no more listening to scratchy vinyl.

In "Help, I'm a Rock," Frank always a little grandiose and self mocking, snubbed
      the sentimental Simon & Garfunkel "I Am a Rock."
In falsetto he sings, "It can't happen here." Of course it could, and it was, and if it
      wasn't, where then might it happen,
in every hair follicle in Kansas, teasing me to join in as I lay on the floor between
      hi-fi speakers.

Thirty years later, at a luncheon held in juvenile detention, I'm losing interest, it's
      not happening here.
I unfold a newspaper laid on a chair, read that the state of Kansas, defined by
      geography not song,
reviewed all bronze roadside historical plaques. State officials decided to remove
      the story of "The Bloody Benders,"
not because on the high prairie a mile northwest of the Mounds and thirteen
      miles from the town
of Parsons where the Bender family built a one room house in 1871, where
      travelers sat for a meal,
they were bludgeoned, robbed, and shoved through a trap door in the floor.
      Eleven bodies,
skulls crushed, unearthed in 1873.

It's not the horrific, not the festering frontier, but Kate, the Bender daughter, the
        "self-proclaimed healer and spiritualist,"
who contacted dead relatives for the locals, who lured men "with a tigerish grace,"
        this "voluptuous girl"
is officially offensive. Death can only be flat and lonely as Kansas. This life of
        heat, humidity, wheat, the official one.
The dead left to God, mass murder to a bronzed plaque. And Frank sings on
        remastered CD's,
"Kansas, Kansas, it can't happen here."

Having a Ball

I never understood the draw
of seeing a giant ball of twine
yet it has defined this town.
Still brings in the curious
to stare and have their picture taken
with its massive, misshapen form.
They laugh and think themselves unique
to pose with hands upon this string
as if they could push it from its shelter
and send it rolling on towards Denver
where years ago (I was in high school),
we were told it could reach.
Once some bastard set the ball on fire.
Townsfolk called for blood but the case
was never solved although the sheriff
was said to know the out of town culprit,
but feared for the kid's life.
The ball was patched and covered up
and life went on and folks calmed down
but a feud later erupted when news reached us
that in a place called Darwin, there was
a bigger twine ball. The sacred book of records
honored us at first, but once the other ball
was measured, we came in second.
So the Twine-a-Thons began
to add size to our famous ball
until we won back the record
and the signs could again read,
"World's Largest Ball of Twine"
without including the shameful "One of The..."
I showed up at the first few Twine-a-Thons
more an excuse to drink beer.
There are those who come out
to pay homage to this ball
that has brought the town fame,
but not fortune, as you can see.
Even add some twine if you need
to feel a kinship to the locals and

this twine god but don't look to do much
shopping as the stores are mostly closed,
or torn down after standing empty
near the great and wondrous ball
which I never understood.

A Kansan Visits New York City

When the neighbor's dog
barks in the rain
at the wind
in the vines of honeysuckle,
you remember the crowd
rippling down Mulberry Street
into Chinatown.
Like leaves on a fence row
they interconnect
and lace
into a rope of green,
an occasional blossom

lifting from the braid.

Oz Revisited

with apologies to L. Frank Baum

Glinda delivers her third child,
and will not return to the stage,
now that exotic dancing no longer
pays, and horny men can see
her strip on the internet.

Munchkins, still the quaint
people, now have satellite TV,
beer and Monday Night Football.
Bored, they bounce in bed
and increase the population.

The Scarecrow finally came out,
and lives quietly with Roger
in Emerald City's East Side,
where he's loved by the locals
for giving so much poetry.

Across from the courthouse,
the statue of Toto, covered with
flying monkey shit, honors
the terrier who was mercifully
put down for complications.

The Tin Man smokes cigars
and tends bar at the Stars & Garter,
spouting homespun philosophy
to anyone who gives a damn.
And few do.

Walking in Tall Weeds

You part the weeds
these thick plants swept
into one rank category
useless or contrary to
the agricultural plan.

Ticks disengage at your
passing warmth and drop on
to a long crawl for blood.
Mosquitos tune you in.
Still you part the weeds.

Chiggers make you
wish your crotch belonged
to someone else.
You must be crazy
but you part the weeds
brushed aside
and closing behind.

Some twich your cuffs
and sign your arms with
tiny marks as swimming
on your feet through
heavy green breath
you part the weeds.

Destination is memory
and time only footsteps
walking in tall weeds.
You reach you.

Driving West

This isn't a poem about the blue clouds
like out of focus angels
that we saw just south of Lawrence,
nor about the way we came up
over the rise east of Manhattan
and found the Flint Hills spread before us --
nor the sunset that carried every bit
of grain and speck of dust
into a silver-edged symphony
of gold and neon, and it's not
the way the dying sun
lit the southwest face
of the grain elevator somewhere past Hays,
exalting it above its workaday self --
not the way the colors feel, the lace border
of black bare branches
backlit by a stripe
of orange sherbet sky,
the lake of blue clouds
like the blue shadows
caught in the drifts of snow
swelling across the prairie.
Instead, this poem is
you and me and Frank and Georgia,
crammed into a
too-small car with too much stuff
arguing the politics of the Civil War
and -- politely, mind you -- taking turns
to sit in the less crowded front seat,
where we can move our feet
without being snarled in blankets
and book bags and the laptop's wires,
driving toward invisible mountains.

Mobile #Twenty-One

West of El Dorado a windmill spins its rusty
flower in an air that might be dreaming Dakota.
A tanker rounds the bend with its flexible load
of fire as new grass deepens a prairie pasture
where forty cows graze, muzzle deep in growth.
A black Baldy raises her face to bawl out a call
for the calf taken from her side. She gets no joy
from her cropping, her big baby hauled off to
Whitewater's feedlot to grow thick in the stink
of a thousand of his kind. The black cow bawls
again, then lowers her head to the new grass.
The tanker shifts gears, wisps of exhaust smoke
trailing away, the sky inhaling the black breath
of the Peterbilt, its fat tires spinning over
the blue trail past the cows to the Whitewater
bridge and west past the feedlot where the calf
noses grain, his hooves splayed in the muck.
A buzzard rides the air that wafts the stink
and spins the windmill's rusty flower and fans
the black cow in her distress west of El Dorado.

Odyssey Through Oberlin

The porcelain insulators are ripe for the picking
(If I only had a ladder and a little more time)
Perched like parakeets along the crossbars
An hour out of Concordia
Westbound on 36
Higley's Home on the Range somewhere off to the right.
But the rusty boxcars are easier to count
As I ponder the question
William Allen White
Sage of Emporia
Put to his readers in an essay
In the August 16, 1896 issue of The Gazette:
"What's the Matter with Kansas?"
Politics aside ... 14, 15, 16, 17
Not a whole lot in my estimation
If I might be allowed to render an opinion
... 18, 19, 20
And at any rate, in Oberlin
I expect to find some answers
... 21, 22, 23
Either at the newspaper office
Home of The Herald
Or huddled around the Great Western
Basking in the warmth of the eight o'clock fire
At my cousin's unpretentious place.
I didn't.
Only the affirmation of answers supplied earlier
In the kind eyes of the Jack-of-all-trades
Who flags me down with a friendly wave
After hearing my right front tire go whap-whap-whap
Over the brick-paved street, then offers to help.
In the sunny smile of the high school girl next door
Who also hears my tire's whap-whap-whap
And springs from the front porch
To join the Jack-of-all-trades,
Then wants to know if I'd like to borrow her cell phone.
In the steady hands of the high school boy (often next door)
Who follows Skinny Jeans to the scene

And is there to pull me up when I trip at the curb
Trying to beat them all to the tire.
Welcome to Oberlin
Red Devils country
Site of the state's last Indian raid.
But today I meet no devils, only angels,
And it's experiences like this –
Just right for packing –
That belong in my bag of memories
As I count my blessings
An hour out of Concordia
Next stop Emporia.

The Deserted Farm

Who leaned the broken mirror
against the barn
knew more than he let on
about the mis-
behavior of moonlight.

Years now since men
left the fields to the luck of foxes,
and left the locks
to rust on unhinged doors.

Still, this last artifice,
this final point of order,
the glass tilted
to survey a weather vane,
the tops of sycamores,

and doubled heaven hung
with chandeliers.

Dust Bowl Diary, 1935

Silt on the dishes.
Rags under the doors.
Horizon coppered by clouds of dirt.
The sun, a dim smear.
No stars, no moon for weeks.
No shadows.

Our farm is sifting away –
only a bit of cornfield stubble
poking up through shifting dunes,
cedars chalked with fine dust,
half-buried fence posts.

Cattle are dying,
their lungs caked with mud.
Others, blinded by blowing grit,
stumble in brown blizzards.

Once my hair shone like corn silk
under the sun. Now it's dull, dry,
wrapped tight in a bun.

After a while, everything
seems the color of vermin,
the color of moths –
dirty wash pinned to
the clothesline,
damp dishcloths
stretched along windowsills.

This spring, no lilacs;
no luster left in Mother's eyes.

I've forgotten the true
colors of things. Even the sky
turns eerie shades I've never seen.
Tonight, before sleep,
I'll lie still
on dusty sheets,
close my swollen eyelids,
and pray for vivid dreams.

Night Sounds

Sounds hang strangely
in the night air, a noisy quiet
that isolates and amplifies.
Breezes tappling in the cottonwoods,
cicadas rasping up and down,
trucks pounding the distant highway,
cars hissing along the street,
a train two miles away picking up speed,
signaling mile crossings,
its receding wall of sound
like background radiation
fading all the way from creation.

A car door slams and signals what—
arrival or departure. Maybe just routine.
Maybe not. Someone's voice,
a laugh the wind distorts,
cries, miserable, repetitive.
The only voice the old woman
across the street
has left after her stroke.

My Boston terrier hovers
in the shadow of a maple's trunk,
head up, ears alert.
I'm standing there too, in the dark,
waiting for him to finish his business
when that strange quality of night sounds
catches in my throat: expectancy.
So much waiting to happen,
temperature falling toward the dew point,
sun circling the planet toward morning,
every day working a degree or two
closer to the equator like a string
wound in a spiral around a stick.
Circumstances turning as on a pivot
toward some inevitable
unimaginable what.

Night Bloom

In awe we watched the flower exist
in its moonlight--a funnel of petal, white
as paper waiting for a word.

Along its vine, seed pods bulged--
round like my belly, that summer
when the baby inside me slept
no better than his brand new parents
in the humid heat of our little home.

So we walked, seeking breeze, and happened
upon a moment whose essence
became part of our story as much
as the preceding springtime's wedding
and our son's birth the following fall.

It's a page I open to again and catch
a glimpse of us holding hands. A new planet
quivers and swells beneath my t-shirt.
We're engulfed in a universe, unknown
as yet, and sweltering

when within our dark uncertainty sweeps
cool perfume, like a scented invitation
from God -- this life, this intimate elixir
could be ours, so we should respond
if we pleased.

Earthfallen

Without the moon the domed sky
deepens and fills with stars, spills

sparks into solid dark
of the windbreak across the field

Tips of light dip, dance
in summer's heat, slip

through rising scent
of dampening soil, through song
of coyotes lifting

through sweep of freedom granted
by night and by desire

standing right here

running barbed wire

under a full twilight moon

an arrow of mallards whistle above

    the clouds slide in

        and line up like ribs

           the sky stretching

                its pied torso

          invites the lover's caress

      to range beyond

    while standing right here

with the cows

Three View of the Deity

The kestrel breaks fast below the lowest
bough of the pear tree, a nestling
in his talons, two kingbirds in pursuit.
And behind them, a raucous jay,
trailing, waiting for a chance.

In front of sun-spoked clouds,
above the too vivid green of the rain-beaten grass,
a cattle egret, blindingly white,
rows in silence through a patch of purest azure.

Below the cry of the kingfisher,
you walk upstream in chest-deep,
fast water, wondering at the foolishness
that led you to this chance and hoping
to make the bank, realizing that water
is the child of the lord whose mother
constantly calls it home.

Past Muster

If you leave the road you die
If you don't leave it who will talk to you
who will hold your hand and step forward
like a flag dipped
in light, a crack
in the sidewalk, the horse
past muster?

from *Things Come On: (an amneoir)*

history becomes fate when
it's over with

no more disjunct
than this world

A gateway timeout occurred
The server / is unreachable

History abounds
a keeling curve
this starts to be how it gets
to keening

love filters   :   red void

Molly's mussels live-o
while she dies-o –
that's the point, see?
                             A space
is a character too

One remembers that, if not what

The space is more historical
than the stars

     *

my mother lives under the ground
so I am drawn to that country

still air cools   water trickles black
roots tower   down   in her house

up here a sky   never whole
buoys around   light of the moon

I could spend half a year   down   where she always lives

It Was Then Our Lives A Little Fire

The destination ahead—
always a piece from a puzzle box.
Those hoses flooding
the pieces I laid as slabs.
After it all— he is put into his bed
as if a knife into a drawer.
We were cattle on our way
to the stockyards on our family vacations
woven as a braided rug
or knitting yarn
in a store window.
Always in his hand
these rough places the car went right over
as if he were God.
Now in his box
in his grave where I could get to him now.

Immigrant Song

Nothing seemed strange
Or bewildering or alien
Besides the wind,
A trace of iron and smoke.

For years I felt the motion
Of our voyage in my limbs.

Even rolling hills
Mirrored waves
Beneath our ship.

When my bones creaked,
It was only rigging
Of sails.

A thunder crack
Was the grizzled captain
Calling us below deck.

As I beckoned to my children
Swimming in grass,
My voice was a gull
Skimming above water.

Then one day I walked
Out the cabin door
Onto a wide grassy beach.

That hill was the ship
Tethered to shore.
The bent oak was the mast.
Cows were shipmates
So grateful for dry land
They lay among rocks
Kissing the earth.

Lunch Time, At Walnut Creek Cemetery

3 miles South, 3½ West, of Glen Elder, KS
September 6, 1978, 7:30 p.m.

We have lunched here for years. A tradition
chiseled from a landmark of bereavement,
an occurrence fixed by circumstance
and coincidence that we farm just across
the road. Today, we are doing it again.
When mother arrives with the food,
she stops by the gate. My brother and I park
our tractors, stretch our backs, and slap
the dust from our hands. Dad and grandpa
join us. Blankets unfurl like parachutes
and sink into the shade of evergreen trees.
We arrange ourselves onto the ground.
Then, just before the first bite of sandwich
or drink of iced-tea or lemonade, mother
does the proper thing and invites the dead
to join us. We discuss her offer and joke
that others might find this odd. We don't care;
this place is comfortable, like a storage room
in an out-of-the-way part of the house
where we choose to open a window.
Fresh air accompanies a music of blue sky,
wind, buffalo grass and weeds --
and a few short rows of tombstones,
shelves lined with preserved points of time.
After lunch, we walk where the deceased
once walked, where neighbor ushered neighbor,
farmer after farmer, into the ground. December 23,
1872 — baby daughter. January 16, 1873 — son,
(same family). August 11, 1891 — dearest
mother. May 3, 1884 — loving wife. March 20,
1880 — kind father. September 6, 1878 — husband.
Infants, children, parents, grandparents,
their lifetimes weathered into ghosts
of assumption, their deaths a mystery.
Scarlet fever? Pneumonia? Diphtheria?

Influenza? Childbirth? The list lingers
with tragedy. Unearthed, a mirage
of settlers idle around us -- pioneers
consumed by a timeless circulation of crops,
plowed fields, and harvests that flow
around these boundaries. After a while,
we all go back to work. From a distance,
I continue to notice the dead. Like long lost
friends, they meander and converse comfortably,
existing on our hospitality, happy
for a momentary taste of resurrection.

breaking the plains

it's not the tractor in the fog,
the faint percussion in the middle ear, muted and dispersed,
popping johnny's progeny, john deere's plowbeam, soil-polished plowshare,
twelvebottom moldboard suited to the plains.
soothing reassurance, stitching air and land, an earthy first fragrance
permeates, loess and loam, gasoline, oiled gunny, sweat and rain.
it's not the moiled light that intervenes, gleams and saturates
the steel, paint and plastic, the wet windshield glass of toyota, audi,
volvo, suburu, chevy and ford parked along the right of way,
the barbed wire fence row of the old oregon trail, where the heavy wagon box
clatters and twists, the loaded axletree and iron-wrapped wheel,
canvas canopies slap, strain and stutter, travel,
jangled chain over ruts, cattle, an ox, a spotted hog in tow.
it's not the gravel road that cuts north along the edge across the draw,
the dormant switchgrass and wild rye that grow in the ditch, crinoidal
limestone shards, mollusk matrices, the sunflower stalks
that ravel, rattle and blow, the indifferent bois d'arc hedge
that spreads tangled offspring into the field.
it's not phlox, sand dropseed, prairie gourd, goldenrod,
mead's milkweed, the fringed orchid, purple clover, queen anne's lace,
squirreltail, needle-leaf sedge, pussy toe, redtop and daisy fleabane.
it's not the distant talkers, the nikon shutter, discussion,
testimony, witness and the awe. it's not john brown, jim lane, quantrill,
speculators, sod busters, border ruffians, jayhawkers,
molasses lappers, exodusters, clod hoppers, not
buffalo, fox, antelope, puma, prairie dog,
mastodon, teleoceras and sabertooth cat.
it's not the kaw.

it's the phantom self-consciously stripping bluestem spikelets to carry home,
the specter in the mirror, the pucker and fold
around the wary green eyes, the well-fed flesh year round, kumquat,
cantaloupe, kohlrabi, artichoke, brown rice, tofu, lox,
pork chop, bacon, leeks, kale and beans.
the face, the curls, the nod, the wistful grin, the deprecatory frown,
protruding ears, the yellow teeth, dull skin growing taut
about the pale forehead, the cheeks and jaw, the chin, the closed skull bones
underneath. frail, transitory. exposed furrow ribs. change.

shape-shifting, form-folding, glacial till, erratic stones,
orogeny, alluvial deposits eroded and washed,
uplift, thrust and fall, settle and fill.
it's you, caught up in this inexorable turning.
not the landscape will not survive, the ocean gone, but you
evolving to the dust that swirls from shears and scatters
in the obscure morning mist.
you drifter in the prairie flux, desperate seizer
of an imaginal razor now.
let loose. you turn the sod.
it's you who drive the plow.

Farmers

plow fields where stories begin
and hope fires more than a flicker
cornered in a kerosene lamp,
burnt in the ache of night,
a place for a soul to grow good
in each man, where no one dies
in the street, but leaves in his sleep,
when the moon lights the way
and crickets announce
his coming to the next life.

Breaking the Drought

Three inches of rain! On the Kansas prairie,
those drowning in dust open their throats.
Listless milo, stunted corn, ragweed

and wild alfalfa stand tall. Only the Western
spruce, backyard survivor of endless high winds,
branches burned brown by waterless skies,

shows no change. Its owner, at ninety twice the age
of her tree, tough as buffalo grass, fragile
as winter wheat at harvest, jokes, "Everything

is half dead and half alive, including me."
The County Agent pokes and pinches, breaks off
brittle twigs, notes how few nodes the tree produced

for spring growth. When he delivers the news --
we could wait and see how it does through winter,
hope for revival -- I'm tempted to agree. But when

my mother says, " Let's cut it down," I understand:
finally, something she can relieve of its suffering,
something that can come to a clear and certain end.

from *Girls on the Roof*

We think of riverbeds as fixed,
carved grooves in the face of the earth,
grooves that make convenient lines
down the middle of maps.
But rivers move, as does the land.
Humans change rivers.
They straighten, dam, and dike them,
building up the water's currents all the more.
Men strip the prairies of grasses
with their long deep roots and
the rivers run even faster.
The rivers will not be tamed.
The wind whipping along the river
will not be tamed.
The fires whipping along the ditches,
the ditches that will fill up with water next spring,
will not be tamed.
Earth, air, fire, water.
Over and over they have their way.
The pull of the river.
The pull of the earth, wind, fire.
What is this thing we call love?
Love is whatever will be missed,
whatever we cannot do without.
Its force cannot be dammed.
It pours out over the land,
turning every house into a boat,
every field into a lake.
You don't know where the river
is anymore and what is underneath.
You have a hint of what lies
behind the bark of a cottonwood tree,
but you're afraid to look toward the horizon.

Cherokee Lessons

I learn the word for bullfrog, *ka-nu-na*,
and remember when we ate frog legs—
ka-nuna gv-tsa-tlv-nv. white meat tender
in batter. *Ka-nu-na a-gwa-du-li.*

Go-dv-nv, crawdads, creep edges
of river shallows, skittering deeper
as I reach. *Go-dv-nv a-na-i.*

Opossums are smiling pigs
under the porch, *si-qua u-tse-tsa-s'di.*
Fairy tales omit these snouted beasts
yet here they lumber through the yard
startling the dogs, teeth protruding.

Sa-li, persimmons, grow nearby.
I learn how *si-qua u-tse-tsa-s'di* climb
their branches to feast. Hunters shake
them to the ground and kick them.

I watch *sa-lo-li*, squirrels. *Sa-lo-li a-na-i.*
They chatter and quarrel all day.

My mother hates the mulberry tree,
gu-wa, because grackles gorge
and drop purple smears on laundry.
I eat its seeded sweetness and know
this summer cosmos has words.

Blackberries

For days I've waited, watched them ripen
through the hot blue afternoons. This morning
I wake dreaming them, waken to a swell
of greed for their taut bodies, those sweet
explosions between roof of mouth and tongue,
the weight of juice poised in my throat.
I creep outside in daybreak's haze,
soles of my feet stealing dew from the lawn;
I'm thinking human, temporal, earthly.
A dove rises flapping and keening
from a nest a foot away, defending two pale eggs
on a bed of twigs. Nothing slows me, I pull
berry after berry from the vine, staining fingertips,
filling my mouth, fervid and wanton, certain
that even in paradise nothing could ever be enough.

At the Museum of Flowers

When I say zinnias do you see them,
Mexico colors, in high Kansas summer
behind the red brick garage? Is your mother
freckling in the sun, holding the green
garden hose gushing water into the bed,
making creamy mud shine like icing?
Do the monarchs light and flutter
from frilled bloom to bloom?
And can you lift them as your father
taught between your first grade fingers,
set one on each shoulder, and
walk into the house wearing wings?

All that summer and deep
into September, will you visit zinnias
hunting for plundered flight?

Tango Trio

A ballroom floor, so dark
not even the slick mirrored surface
reflects a pinpoint of starlight.
Three dancers night blind
to their delicate feet, only feeling
supple boots that caress their toes.
Partners gone or never come,
three women prepare to dance
their becoming into lithe being,
to tango with pencil, keyboard,
leaking pens trailing black vines
of revision and uncertainty.

At round tables, white paper orbs
filled with flames that echo the music
illuminate those restless circling satellites,
an audience insatiable for blood,
drama or explosion, wanting every stroke
of rough graphite to annihilate boredom.

But it's only tango, and three women
dancing as sinuously as they can,
with all the grace they have left
after their day scalps them,
minds raw and churning with ideas
they can't trap in the Tupperware
they're either filling or washing
or putting away, power swirling
around and out the stainless steel
kitchen sink, the stove burning
imagination to a lump of cinder,
work kidnapping their clave heartbeats,
lost on the long commute
as they listen to audio books
they could have written.

Kissing Bea on the Prairie

Bea tells me to turn off the road
at a silo in a part of Leoti
she does not know. The prairie grasses
around us move as an ear on a cat would
to listen, the way stalks on sunflowers tilt
to put sun in their seeds and petals.
It is dark--the shade of well water,
and the stars are not ours, but we see them
up there, like sequins on a black dress.
Bea takes off her underwear,
and it falls into the heather. I take off
her shirt, and my hands hold her
as if it is my first time, my fingers
like rain that runs over the body
rather than falling upon it.
Her shirt and bra go
to my car hood, and her knee
is at my belt loop, and the car lights come
down that long dirt road and speed by.
Then, the dark Camero backs up,
and we are in our car, too, being chased
into town. All I have known
are the suburbs with their street signs
and traffic lights, and their waxed police cruisers
on nearly every corner, and then
there is Bea, a prairie girl; I've known her only five months,
and the land that brought her up: the heather
in autumn, the valleys that hold a little water
at their bases, and the sparse shelter belts that call in the birds.
We beat the other car into town, and it turns,
and vanishes, and we wonder if that was their land--
if they chased us for violence or sport. I rest
my hand on Bea's thigh, and we quit thinking, quit
speaking, and kiss.

Cicadas in August

She weeds the humid green as
August heat leans in, finding milkweed
feebler than its own roots; failing again
and again to unlock the ground around
a milky stem as all around her those cicadas,

their love calls gnaw the evening air: It isn't
fair, the way it ends so soon, a lifetime
of waiting and a hope
that sprouts wings. Nothing
is ever enough. And yet that sound,

the pure desire in it is something, is more
than can be had by a woman in hiding;
she knows, and still, daily, she fortifies
her life against that heat, the smell and feel
of invaders. But sometimes

in the night   something   a picture
or a word   creeps into her
dreams   moves over her bare skin
light as moths   something possible
stirs beneath that clay and then

vanishes the moment she opens
her eyes. And she moves
through the heat of a new day,
keeping her eyes open, running
her hands over her arms, almost
remembering, thinking she hears it
again in the elms that sway
above her quiet house
in her waking hours.

Vanguard

Here's what I remember: Coleman Hawkins
and I are sitting at a mahogany table
in the Village Vanguard, quietly talking.
He's finished a set in which he was unable
to summon even one unbroken tone
from the bell of his once-clarion saxophone.
But now that's over and he feels all right.
He's smoking because he's wanted to all night,
drinking cloudy cognac from a tumbler
and coughing ferociously; his voice is weaker
than his cough; he's barely audible, mumbling
to me because he knows I'm from Topeka.
He says, "That's where I learned to tongue my horn."
I know, and that's the only thing I hear.
        It's 1969; in half a year
he'll be dead. In three years I'll be born.

The Leaver

The crabapple Kansas of sixteen ran me mad,
ran me away from the flatness and fleeting
green, ran me to the woman, St. Theresa,
the cherub-faced social worker, who I would meet
much later, mid-twenties. She held the same promise
of an unborn child, the promise that in the end
all becomes dirt. There were women to love,
but only if I could confuse love
with its opposite, and only if the women were fine
believing the lies we lay down to create, lies like whispers
of ourselves reflected in our glisten and sheen.
I met illness too. For me,
cancer. But what is all of this to Kansas?

What of St. Theresa, who sold a cocaine death,
who sold addiction and called it artistry,
who etched the minutes in my face
like years, who tried to feed me and fill the hole
left from losing those childhood
plains? Does Kansas miss
the leaver, and will Kansas keep me
if I return? You will never know
my Kansas, never know its summer song
sung over wheat, whistled by wind, the hollering promise
of salvation for those of us trying to crawl our way back.
Kansas can never be home until it has been lost.

The Perfect Poem

would say only the words
sun and stone, stream and tree
and earth, yet it would explain
what I know of home
standing in late summer's
hazy evening light, dust rising
and settling on this road,
under the smell of cottonwoods,
the last of the day's
sun on this heart-shaped
leaf in my hand.

It would say only
the words fire
and flood, wind
and grass, yet
would capture my surprise
each spring at the turning in
of the compost,
last summer's onion stalks,
cucumber skins, and grass clippings
now dirt. Stirred
in the wet heat
of last August and broken
by worms and coffin cutters,
they have all become again
that which they were,
the perfect poem.

After Driving Cattle in the Flint Hills

Tallgrass tangled in stirrups.
Cowhands leaning on long shadows.
After all these years,
I am still in love.

Autumn

Begin Again

Little Hawk

There was a man once
called Swoop of a Bird.
I am not the only one
who has flown to your

dance with air
urgent song lifting those
lowdown roadside clouds.
The eye that sees

weeps a dark comma
and swiftly goes.
You have been sweeter
than I deserved.

Take Memory Lightly

To re- member, to populate your life again,
with the past may not be clarity.
The Great Plains, the Prairie, appears to be
a sea of endless nothingness,
without life.
After 20 miles of plains, a tree
becomes a green miracle. Look!
A tree! A tree in the emptiness.

Then, instead of seeing the flicker of red
like new-minted fire in the witchgrass,
or the trailing robe of the wind
crossing the road just ahead of you,
a low, yellow brown mist of dust,
we strain to see another tree,
the memory of Tree clouding our vision.
The memory creating a need in the now.
And the now:
the wind, the witch grass,
the never looking up to see the hawk
is lost.

Notes on the Journey

The road is just a road,
be it a rut carved in the
wind-flayed grass
or a sticky blacktop finger
pointing to the horizon.

The road is just a road,
under blistered soles
or bald tires or
(more likely) both
at the same time.

The road is just a road -
it's not the sad filling station oasis
squatting beside it;
it's not the glittering ocean
or bleak cliff beyond it;
it's not even the ghosts
that pierce it at regular
intervals, like mile markers,
like buoys of hope
and umpteenth chances and
rusted-shut dreams.

The road is just a road,
second cousin to
the churning ship wake,
a reflection of the airplane
tracks that zipper
the forgiving sky.

The road is just a road,
and it goes three ways:
where you've always been
and where you could be,
but mostly where you
are, right now.

Indian Summer

Tonight you were on the bench,
lining your knees up with mine.
It was familiar - so much
like other times when
we counted minutes
under umbrellas,
across the table, or over
railings. This night
you were wistful, a creeping vine
winding into my cracks.
"I am hoping for frost,"
you said, and I watched
the first leaf fall.
I let your head drop
to my collar and felt
a trembling sigh
radiate from your bones.
The swelter of August was receding;
the chill came in.

Between the Fall Grass

and the fox's cry—
like a woman screaming—
I hear the owl walk sideways on the branch
of the Mugo Pine
I cut down two summers past,
taken by bark beetles
and burnt that winter. Things are changing.
I can hear them in the smoke steps
of an owl who flew
into the tree, not seeing
me in the screen porch, almost
asleep in the gloaming,
in the movement of beetles
I almost hear in the pine.
      Then the fox,
one field west, its cry
frightening enough for me to cross
the road first time I heard it,
sure some neighbor or poor traveler
was meeting red death
in green summer's grass. Now,
Then, I watched the owl,
who too had heard it all before,
shift himself, then
let loose his own great hoot,
as underneath him, beetles
took a better hold, and time
had its ways with us.

Spiritus Mundi

Listen around to the long sentence the land is saying,
to the wind rumoring through the aggregate of grasses.

Hear the soft explosions of all that is tilled under,
a scumble of clods cleaved by the blade, the sheared leavings

of wheat, and memory, memory, a root system still
drilling down, searching out moisture, anything that's useful,

anything dear. Do you recognize your own shy gestures
in the weft of the fields? Oh sisters and brothers,

let the gentle tether of our longing keep us here
among the undulant, amber barley and russet oats.

And if all flesh is grass, then let us live humbly, as grasses do.
In sympathy, we shall shiver and bend, pressing our knees

into the earth, turning our faces to the quavering sun

Hiawatha

In late October
when the full moon
shines over Hiawatha
in the early evening

trucks line up under the grain elevator
like children waiting for Halloween candy
at the home of a good neighbor.

People walk like ghosts
under rows of maple trees.

And grain comes down
like manna
and candy
and the full moon

and the leaves
of the maples
fall.

Here in Topeka

In a neighborhood of old shade, maple seeds helix down,
        winging onto windshields, mixing
with the berry-smeared shit of birds and clotting the gutters.

        From this wide porch of the Middle West
one can hear supper plates clatter and the responsible hum
        of leafblowers. It's the dog-walking hour

when screen doors bang and the neighbor's ex drives past,
        bass strafing the place. He's just trying
to get a look at his kid on the way to his railyard shift.

        Amid the iteration of American four-squares
and airplane bungalows, the people of this town are coupled up
        and hunkering down. Here the weathervane

has rusted east, pointing toward the statehouse, where books
        first happened to young Langston Hughes,
and in Curry's famous mural, sulphurous clouds muscle above

        John Brown's fierce Bible and rifle stance,
fire flagging at his back, blood and the dead under his boots.
        When streetlamps judder on, it's time to go in

to the placid tones of the local newscaster's evening report
        on the usual city council incivilities.
The radar forecasts what the wind chimes already know.

What This Town (Lawrence) Needs Is More Monks

1
Not trying to be all uppity about it
Just a notion and wonder if
You could ever get used to living
Across the street from a wat

2
Just the least bit of something
Passing by in a line
Them again this time with bowls
Looking for rice from the women
On the block
Nice touch to dawn

3
One thing for sure
There are more gongs than guns
In Laos and even though
The USA tried mighty hard to introduce
Military hardware into the culture
They failed and it is obvious why
Gongs are followed by prayers

4
We met a woman
As we walked in a lane
We asked her what she had been
Doing at the temple?
"Putting up lights!" was her answer
And there was no reason at all to ask
Any more
Questions.

5
The sudden realization that
the ones in white
Are nuns…
Not exactly enlightnenment
Almost but not quite the same

6
They appear quite suddenly
Standing next to and a step
Above you
Asking in English
Where you come from
As if you were more
Interesting and important
Than the statue of Bhudda
We are all leaning on.

7
The woman was
walking her cow through
the wat
they both appeared to
be engaged with the monks
without getting all
charismatic
about it

8
the teenage monk
invited us to prayers
come when the gong gongs
sit in the back
don't say anything
we don't mind

(a wat is a temple in Cambodia, Thailand, or Laos)

Picking Pumpkins

We cross the levy to find the vines,
wringing the handles of sickles
with garden-gloved hands.
Rows of sprouts, patched into
well-drained soil, carve rectangle
fields into the ground.
The ribs of pumpkins flare,
each one its own puffed chest
huddled against splintered stems.
My grandpa works with a scythe,
bending his body at the waist
on fake hips that crackle like bonfires,
his face warped in the sunlight.
I sneak cigarettes behind the pick-up,
each breath a mix of rotting pulp,
tobacco, and pumpkin seeds.
The meat of my thumbs ache
from cutting stems.
Grandma and grandpa lean
against the wind, failing plant stems,
blossoms cut from the tips. The autumn gold,
bushkin, cheese pumpkin, are always ready
for carving and cutting from the vine,
We leave the place greened, weeded.
Even big moons cave in our tired palms.
We fill our shirts and buckets
with sugar treats, winter luxuries.
These baby pumpkins know
how to live and die quietly,
sitting on window ledges till
mid-November, faceless.

A Feast of Cheap Tacos

In the courtroom where everything
is dissolved she swears to tell
the truth the whole truth about division
of assets, of debt, of child,
of two people too
different to reconcile.

Among gleaming
wooden walls and government seals
and the honorable this
and that, a half-shaded window
gazes outside at cars driving about, to work,
to the store, to appointments. She remembers

not the day she stood in a field bright with dying sun
wearing a red dress and pearls, the promises
of faith, of trust, of love, of course love,
and the slide of old rings onto trembling fingers. Not that.

She remembers years
earlier, coming home and sprawling on the bed
with him, with a feast of cheap
tacos, propping pillows around
her growing belly-child. She held his face
in both hands. They were so hungry,
and there was so much food.

Still Life With Dirty Dishes

The problem is, how to paint this so it looks beautiful—
because I know it must seem like any other sink
full of dishes. Maybe worse.
Avocado shells float through the wreckage
of lunch, bright orange macaroni clings to plates
jutting out amid half-hearted suds, and some pale
bloated noodles met their watery grave already
sunken below in a tangle of forks.
But you see, these dirty dishes
are the picture of time I didn't spend
washing them, time spent instead
this afternoon on the couch, arms full
of napping daughters.
The three of us, combined like a crayon creature
my toddler would draw—three heads,
three pairs of arms and legs,
sprawling and intertwined.
I held my children there for hours
in the stillness of their sleep, wondering
what colors their dreams were.
Iridescent, maybe tropical I guessed
as I watched their eyelids flutter
like the fins of tiny fish.

Pecan Picking

Everything on the ground is the color
of tree bark. My earth-coated fingertips
are my eyes, sifting through cracked
leaves, pausing at every smooth pecan.

Even while sprawled on a picnic blanket,
my spine arched like a seal's, this work
feels primitive, as if a family's survival
depends on my filling one bucket, then another.

The bluest sky in weeks overhead,
I am too busy for worries or even dreams.

October Night

Light stops
like a clock.
Fallen leaves confess to shoes
while mice mumble communion prayers
up and down fields of alfalfa.
As Andromeda bends over for a good-night kiss
her dark hair cascades into our eyes.
She tucks us into the night
and the moon shows her
what we have become--
shadows on the prairie.

1942

Standing.
Close enough to feel
the fresh turned gravel
through my thin-soled shoes.
No fake grass to obscure
the reality of that bare hole.
Rifles popped and echoed.
A far away bugle gave us
the saddest of all Amens,
which chilled and chilled.
My father shuddered
and pulled me close.
Embarrassed and ashamed for him,
I watched tear drops leave his eyes
to fall on that ground
which was only beginning to show
its insatiable hunger
for the young men of our town.

Somewhere Near Abilene

"G. H." . . . a Kansas artist . . .
Somewhere near Abilene,
Took canvas, paint, and strips of wood,
And conjured up a scene
That hangs on our living room wall.

Not every day,
But when I'm in the mood,
That painting takes my eye
Into that Kansas scene,
Somewhere near Abilene.

Does the power lie
In color, form, or texture?
Strips of cedar, glued onto canvas,
For clouds, and trees, and fence—
Then all painted one golden color.

No . . . look closer . . .
It just seems one color,
But the color is what first catches the eye,
Shades of yellow, brown, and gold,
For both Kansas sky and prairie grass,
As if reflecting one another,
Then merging . . . becoming one . . .
At the horizon.

But in that prairie grass . . . there . . .
See . . . a touch of green.
If the sun were setting just right,
Off there in the distance,
Just below that lost horizon,
Reflecting off of those cedar chip clouds,
It might then imbue everything—
Sky, and trees, and grass—
With its own golden color.

You can imagine such a scene . . .
Somewhere near Abilene.

But aren't these shapes too surreal?
Trees that cannot be trees,
Strips of wood, glued to canvas
The large one on the left,
On this side of the fence,
A tree or a cactus plant?
In Kansas . . . it must be a tree . . .
But a strip of wood . . .
Like the fence, like the clouds.
That smaller tree,
Further away, far beyond the fence,
Less distinct in the distance,
May be more believable,
As stylized as the clouds.
Still, I've seen those weathered trees . . .
Haven't I?
Somewhere near Abilene?

The fence may be the secret.
Those strips of wood,
Posts and rails,
Do look like a fence,
A fence that might be found
Somewhere near Abilene,
Running off to the horizon,
Running off into that sunset,
Getting smaller and smaller until it disappears,
Having found another dimension for the spirit
Out there on that open prairie.

That's what holds my imagination.
I step into that scene,
To lean against that fence,
Contemplate that sunset,
Then walk on down that fence line . . .
Walk out of sight,
Into that other dimension,
Somewhere near Abilene

Questions of Travel On Route 66

for Elizabeth Bishop

When you read poems, who could resist
all the cleverly split ends you went
to and oh! through such means: chains
of silver spectacles; a sprig of lilacs
at your throat, as effective as garlic
for putting off the strangers of Chicago;
a long arm of wit that might launch ships
or fleets of floating words, phantom
holographs, keeper at home of the oddest
small things come to roost. What dreams
are you guide to that drive me farther
from heaven, hell, and everything between?
Far off details stall or circle like magic
lantern scenes: ground fog shimmers
like a scrim. Like a figure in a shroud,
a hooded, grey sweatshirted farmer
farms his tract, his tractor burning,
his brand upon the gate. The sun,
a hot pink fire balloon, flares out,
bursting gold seams in the satin clouds.
This last is alchemy, but I see now where
it's going -- not this simple machinery,
not this journey, not this masque,
not the point of this or any metaphor
but the way itself, a vanishing point
opposite yours, like that half twist
in a Möbius strip where all at once
a pencil line is drawn into infinity.
How's that work? Magic words? Something
up your sleeve, silky-smooth as a scarf,
nothing shown, nothing given away, just
your touch. Anyone can pluck a white hare
out of a hat. Now, how can I change scars
into stars, make spring eternal paradise
again, love life, bait a better snaketrap,
save my own skin this fall? Look at these

stars! Constellations of migrating geese
rise out of the north and off you fly, back
down to the land of crocodiles, dolphins,
crabs, armadillos, puffins, cocks, and awks.
I keep dogs in my yard. Nerval had a lobster
on a leash. It knew the secrets of the sea
and didn't bark. Now, there's something
to be said for the art of surprise.
Just how many miracles will I need?
I see you twist the tail on every (p)ink pig
in a pen, smoke out ears from my fields
like an inflammable ghost, parting the gold
stalks, row and row, the halves sliding
almost together behind on the blacktop,
so hot all I see's a mirage. The red-
winged blackbird on his fencepost turns
to land in that lake, crying and crying
after us, invaders in his territory.
In your wake, I take trips, wear hats,
watch as frogs and farmers disappear.

The Call

The harvest is past, the summer
Is ended, and we are not saved.
-Jeremiah 8:20

The morning before it happens
at the rim of the field I wait
for the call: the hard ground,
the lull, and all around, on the verge
the lit houses lie sorted and stored.
And now the sound of arrowheads
without shafts scything through a field
making room for ripe new fruit. A
shudder. Then no sound. Some people
live out their entire lives.
It was hard to imagine when you
came here all you wanted was
his smile. Now you can dance,
busy yourself getting old. So hard to
leave the faded heaven, unwritten letters,
contagions, the lies, hedging possibility,
simple absence, warped miracle.
The morning before it happens
at the rim of the field I wait
for the call: it's possible
to hear distant apples drop
against the answer of such air, to
follow that sound till you find
no apple and no tree. The flesh
has dissolved into secret;
the bones are in the sea.

On Receiving the Key to Unit F-25

This November
has been as mismatched
as my funeral suit.

The chill air
came to claim me
and the free wine
tried to fight it off.

And I have not slept
in days when someone hands me
a box of belongings:

artifacts of a lost
civilization
that I had only seen
the ruins of in you.

And your foul breath preserved
in blues harp after blues harp,
these harmonicas wheezing
your way back into the world
these exhalations you'd saved without knowing it.

And now your sons
wonder about you.
I wonder about that man
who'd gone so wrong.

What hard things
had calloused your demeanor
while your hands remained

so tender,
so surprisingly steady,
with a good pencil clenched
between these same fingers I've inherited.

You remained to the last
a conjurer of images, images
almost shockingly whimsical
in your private ossuary
your personal frownland, which I cannot go back to.

Your cabinet of curiosities
whose doors have now been closed,
whose guts now sit in a storage unit,
placed there by hands more sure than mine.

Now all I can do
is plunk out shaking
some song on the piano
that I'm pretty sure you hated

and otherwise occupy myself
with my destructive love, destructive
in a different way than yours was.

Here I am in my current apartment,
my walls so sparse, babysitting a furnace
that doesn't like to stay lit

with no sackcloth or ashes.
The ashes I've refused.
          They are not you.

Nobody Wants to Write An Elegy

You would do anything to avoid that
You just want one more day with dad
Watching Turner Classics together
Talking about the old days
Talking about Canada
Talking about the Union Pacific Railroad
Talking about being broke and on the road with the band
Talking about mother
Gone almost ten years
He still misses her
"I would be so glad if she
Just walked through that door, son"
The next movie
Brings him back to his early
Teens when he was an usher
In one of those grand movie palaces
In Calgary
He begins to gets away from me
Walking toward the screen
In his majestic
Almost military uniform
He disappears from the
Room

He is gone

Nobody wants to write an elegy
You would do anything to avoid that
Everybody wants just one more day

Elkins Prairie

Humans were generated under this condition, that they
watch over that globe , called Earth, which you see in the
center of this sacred region; and they were given souls
from the sempiternal fires called stars, those spherical
divine intelligences that complete their orbits with
awesome speed.   —*Cicero, Somnium Scipionis*

1
Drove out to Elkins Prairie last night
to see the ploughed and broken earth
by moon and starlight.
                                        The windbeaten tree
was invisible from the roadside.
Had they ploughed that under too
with the milkweed and fringed orchid?
I wanted that symbol of defiance
to be there still, and thought,
Is it too late for us? I remembered
Horace, who thought his Italian countryside
was too far gone, and Vergil, who warned
his countrymen to take thought
before cleaving virgin prairie with iron.
All the earth is sacred, and heaven is contained
in every particle of soil, but humans,
whose very name means sod, and who
were generated from the dust of stars
to care for this little globe of earth,
have long forgotten.
                                Above the darkened land
the Goat Star was rising with her Kids.
Higher up, the Pleiades and Mars, the god of fields,
studded the shoulder of Taurus,
and higher still, the barren gibbous Moon
was swinging across the late November sky.

2
Ken had been working for years to save it
and so we were out there in the mist
clambering through the rough furrows,
my ten year old son holding the flashlight
as we loaded pieces of dying sod into bags
and slung them into the trunk of the car
to be replanted later in our backyard gardens.
(continued, stanza break)

On the drive back my son wanted to know
is this stealing, and the adults explained
the owner had rights to the property
but not to the prairie, that sometimes
the precepts were closed
and sometimes they were open,
that we were trying to keep alive
a little piece of what someone had hurt,

hoping the words made as much sense
as the feel and smell of the rooted dirt.

3
a small patch
of dense coarse
grasses brown
grays and green

placed in the
mulched garden,
hose water
circling, chant

the dharani,
protect this land
from hungry
ghosts roaming.

Fog

The faded, sometimes missing line
at the highway's edge conspires this morning
with fog, a moving dome of uncertainty,
and the muscle in my chest that clenches

and relaxes tamely now but picks
secret reasons and moments to race,
bored by its mundane life, its narrow
choices: beat day and night. Or stop.

Nurses plug their patients into machines—
we are piecework—collect their printouts,
and the shiny doctor descends, thumps,
taps, listens, says, "Take your pulse often."

As in the song, I think, "Keep a close watch,"
but don't say it, and shut the doors gently
so not to alarm the hovering fog.

Rebuilding Year

After Beloit I went back to the paper
and wrote arts features for eight dollars an hour,
and lived in the Gem Building, on the block between
Topeka High with its Gothic tower
and the disheveled Statehouse with its green
dome of oxidizing copper.

I was sorry that I had no view
of old First National. Something obscured it
from my inset balcony. I heard it
imploding, though, like Kansas Avenue
clearing its throat, and saw the gaudy brown
dust-edifice that went up when it came down.

Friday nights I walked to High's home games
and sat high in the bleachers,
and tried to look like a self-knowing new
student, and tried not to see my teachers,
and picked out players with familiar names
and told them what to do.

Finding the Scarf

The woods are the book
we read over and over as children.
Now trees lie at angles, felled
by lightning, torn by tornados,
silvered trunks turning back

to earth. Late November light
slants through the oaks
as our small parade, father, mother, child,
shushes along, the wind searching treetops
for the last leaf. Childhood lies

on the forest floor, not evergreen
but oaken, its branches latched
to a graying sky. Here is the scarf
we left years ago like a bookmark,

meaning to return the next day,
having just turned our heads
toward a noise in the bushes,
toward the dinnerbell in the distance,

toward what we knew and did not know
we knew, in the spreading twilight
that returns changed to a changed place.

Bittersweet Season

Colors have faded
from red maple leaves
and bronze chrysanthemums.
Even mornings pale.

We drive down country roads
silent of birdsong,
streams dried to ditches,
barns shambled in fields.

sit in narrow living rooms,
ashes cold in fireplaces,
dress in drab flannel shirts,

steep tea, let it grow cold,
nibble dry toast,
burn candle stubs.

Our lives turn brittle.
Foreheads ache
against moonless nights.

On a last walk before winter
we button our coats
against November
find a tangle of bittersweet still alive.

Frontier Bride

First year of marriage
in a one-room cabin on the prairie,
and for weeks on end it blows –
whirring at the windowsills,
rattling the walls, bending the creek willows,
billowing my skirts. Endless
gusts of wind I hear with each whipstitch,
with every broom sweep,
constant as my own
breath, whimpering around
the doors of my dreams until I want
to slam them shut. Only
sometimes, late at night
with him, a blessed hush,
when – wedding quilt slipped to the floor,
head thrown back, hair a silky tangle,
orange sickle of moon curving
through the window –
I'm lost
in love wild
as an autumn field.

This Day

If this day should be my last,
it has been a satisfaction:
coffee climbing the percolator's stem,
blue smell of plums,
sunlight fueling an orange.
At dusk, a crow calls and calls my name,
night subtracting its wings.

Ode to Bill Stafford

Your poems were never to a set agenda.
What words people marveled at
You put aside, for what others might call
Mundane, out of place, too ordinary.
All too available.

Every morning at five
You the explorer, put on
Your gray shirt, khakis, and shoes
And went in search,
Not of a poem

But the first faint call
Of a fish hook glinting dull in the mud,
A lost country on a wall where
Ants pass on the right,
Black hats with voices
That ride our thoughts.

You the explorer with the dull
Glinting hook, did not throw it away
For lack of promise.
You held fast instead and listened
To its real music,
And danced along the shore.

You became a flute-player,
Father of fish, and they
Hearing the melody
Dance onto the shore
With their fish legs after you
Twisting their fish bodies
Doing the holy wiggle.

You, the explorer, gave your
Gray shirt and khaki pant
To the lead fish – still dancing –
And walked into a high cabin
White from the sanctity
And your sister waiting

With scarves and gloves
Laughs at you because she knows
You've been dancing with the fish
To a melody all too forgotten.

How strange that we laugh at your explorer ways
How you go out in search of nothing
And come back complete,
With ants, fish, deer,
Black hats, white suits, a war camp,
Dead people, a lost country.

How is it that for us that come after you
Your music is old.
Must poems come from grand ideas?
We are so intellectual.
We forget sometimes the best
Lesson is the complaint of birds.

And your sister,
Waiting, steps onto the hard
Snow-covered ground
Fastens dogs to the sled
And waits for you to come out
Decked in winter gear.

Father explorer,
What will you find?

Threads in the snow reaching
Deep into our silence?
White horses dead
In front of your sled?

This morning I found your shirt
And khakis, well washed,
Hanging on the gray branch of a tree,
The hook, anchored to the front right pocket,
Still glinting dull.

Blue Brick From the Midwest

After my father collapsed like a bolt of light, toppled without a word,
I was the one to enter his study, find the jagged note to our mother he
scratched as he reeled, the freight train of his departure hurtling
through his heart—

and
all
my
love

—a sentiment he did not speak in 79 years as tough customer,
affable but stern, inert when grief came, reserved as granite
when my brother died, cracking plaintive jokes when we trembled
in the hospital, mother going under the knife.

His way was trenchant, oblique. He distrusted those who
talk about God, preferring to honor the holy with a glance,
a nod, or silence. Delving deeper, the day he died, we found
in his sock drawer, under that scant set of flimsy raiment, the fetching
photo of the flirt: our mother, coy at the sink, looking back
over her shoulder, dressed only in an apron with a big bow.
No fool like an old fool.

And delving deeper, at the back of the bottom file (the niche
where one would hide the stuff of blackmail) I touched the blue
brick of love letters our mother had sent him when they
courted in the war—brittle leaves kissed snug together
and bound with string, the trove he had carried
in secret through every move since 1943. She knew
them not, nor had his. "Oh, Billy," she said.

Father, early years taught your way with the heart's contraband
when the dirty thirties blunted your bravado, tornado snatched
your friends, the war your tenderness, and left you with these secrets
hoarded for us to find when you were gone.

Assurance

You will never be alone, you hear so deep
a sound when autumn comes. Yellow
pulls across the hills and thrums,
or the silence after lightning before it says
its names – and then the clouds' wide-mouthed
apologies. You were aimed from birth:
you will never be alone. Rain
will come, a gutter filled, an Amazon,
long aisles – you never heard so deep a sound,
moss on rock, and years. You turn your head –
that's what the silence meant: you're not alone.
The whole wide world pours down.

Contributors

Lorraine Achey, a life-long autodidact, has studied subjects ranging from anatomy & physiology to Zimbabwean mbira. Poetry writing started with her sixth grade teacher's encouragement, and has continued with varying success over the years. She also writes for her personal and business blogs, and recently sent her first poetry collection, *Diner on Dark's Last Corner* in search of a publisher. Lorraine has lived quietly with the stark beauty of the prairie of southwest Missouri/southeast Kansas all her life, and shares her home with three dynamic "Diva Dogs." She works as a massage therapist when she is not reading, writing, or grooming dogs. www.floodgaps.blogspot.com.

Abayomi Animashaun is a Nigerian emigre whose poems have appeared in such journals as *Diode, Drunkenboat, African American Review,* and *Southern Indiana Review.* He is the winner of the 2008 Hudson prize and a recipient of a grant from the International Center for Writing and Translation. Animashaun's poetry collection, *The Giving of Pears,* is available through Black Lawrence Press. www. abayomianimashaun.com

Marie Asner is an entertainment reviewer in the greater Kansas City area and with Chicago outlets. She has had regular appearances on KCUR-FM (Kansas City NPR). Marie is a free lance writer, poet, workshop presenter and past member of Kansas Arts on Tour. She is a contributor to the Last Book project with displays in Buenos Aires, Zurich and New York City. www.kansaspoets.com/ks_poets/asner_marie.htm

Jackie Magnuson Ash grew up on a farm in central Kansas, later to return to raise two children and help her husband manage the farm business. She holds an English degree from Emporia State University and is a member of Prairie Poets and Writers, a Salina group which self-published its work in *PlainSpoken: Chosen Lives, Chosen Words.*

Anne Baber's poetry has appeared in *Kansas City Voices* and on a Grammy-*nominated CD and been recognized by The Ontario Poetry Society,* The Writer's Digest November 2009 Poem-A-Day Challenge,

and The Saturday Writers Guild. Her first Chapbook, *Endless,* was published by Finishing Line Press in 2011.

Walter Bargen has published thirteen books of poetry and two chapbooks. The latest are: *The Feast,* BkMk Press-UMKC, 2004, winner of the 2005 William Rockhill Nelson Award; *Remedies for Vertigo* (2006) from WordTech Communications; *West of West* from Timberline and *Theban Traffic* (2008) WordTech Communications. In 2009, BkMk Press-UMKC published *Days Like This Are Necessary: New & Selected Poems.* He was appointed to be the first poet laureate of Missouri (2008-2009).

K. L. Barron has a weakness for landscapes, Kansas being the most enduring. She lives in the Flint Hills and teaches literature and writing at Washburn University. She's published poems, fiction and non-fiction in *New Letters, The Bennington Review, Midwest Quarterly, The Little Balkans Review,* and *Chickenbones et al.*

Roy J. Beckemeyer, a retired aeronautical engineer from Wichita, studies fossils insects that lived in Kansas 250 million years ago, and edits two scientific journals. He has been writing poetry since he sent his first love poem to his high school sweetheart, Pat, now his wife of fifty years. www.windsofkansas.com.

Allison Berry was born and raised in Pittsburg, Kansas. She received her bachelor's degree from Cornell College and her master's from Pittsburg State University. She lives in Pittsburg with her wife and son, and she teaches English and Women's studies at Pittsburg State University.

Elizabeth Black grew up on a farm in southwest Kansas. After a long career as a teacher, writer, journalist, and editor in the Washington D.C. area, she moved to Lawrence, Kansas in 2007. Elizabeth is the author of the novel *Buffalo Spirits,* which drew on her experiences growing up in western Kansas. www.ElizabethBlack.com.

Lori Brack's work has appeared in *The Packingtown Review, North American Review, Another Chicago Magazine, Rosebud,* and other journals.

Her first chapbook *A Fine Place to See the Sky*, a poetic script written as a collaboration with her grandfather's 1917-1922 Kansas farming journals for a work of performance art with artist Ernesto Pujol, was published in 2010.

Mickey Cesar is a former soldier and sailor who lives in Lawrence, Kansas, with his cat Carmen. He is the author of two full-length poetry collections, *Vanishing Point* (219 Press, 2005) and *If I Were On Fire* (Spartan Press, 2011). He holds an MFA in Creative Writing from the University of Kansas. www.mickeycesar.com

Victor Contoski enjoys retirement to no end, working currently on a long sequence of short dream poems and a manuscript of his adventures at the Monroe Institute, detailing spiritual exploration. He is also working with Jolene Anderson on a book on spiritual awakenings. His poetry books include *Midwestern Buildings* and *Broken Treaties*.

Maril Crabtree has lived in Kansas most of her adult life. Her poems are published in *Coal City Review, Flint Hills Review, Steam Ticket, Kalliope, New Works Review* and others. She is Poetry Co-editor of *Kansas City Voices*. Her most recent chapbook is *Moving On* (Pudding House Press, 2010). www.marilcrabtree.com.

Daniele Cunningham's poetry is informed by Zen ethics, which she grounds with images of place, particularly the landscapes of Kansas. Her poetry has been published in the *Cow Creek Review*, the *SEK Celebration Program*, and has been the focus of her thesis for a Master of Arts in English at Pittsburg State University. www.danielewrites.blogspot.com and www.danielecunningham.com

Rebekah Curry's primary qualifications are having lived in the state for over sixteen years and having made attempts at poetry for over ten. She is currently a student at the University of Kansas, where she is majoring in Classics.

Brian Daldorph teaches at the University of Kansas and Douglas County Jail. He edits *Coal City Review*. His latest collection of poems: *Jail Time* (Original Plus P, 2009).

Jan Duncan O'Neal, after a twenty-year career in librarianship, retired to Overland Park where she writes poetry. Her work has appeared in *I-70 Review, The Mid-America Poetry Review, Thorny Locust* and *Coal City Review*. She has written eleven language arts resource books for teachers. Jan has done storytelling workshops in 25 states. She is currently an editor for *I-70 Review*. Her chapbook, *Voices: Lost and Found,* will be published in autumn 2011 by The Lives You Touch Publications.

Eric Dutton has done all of the big things in Kansas: he was born there, educated there, married and divorced there. He became a father there. He says "there" because he lives in Florida now, but Kansas will always be a "here" for him.

Paula Glover Ebert is an English graduate student at Kansas State University. A native of Colorado, she spent 30 years as a journalist in Colorado and Wyoming before coming to Kansas. She is recently married to a farmer who works his family farm outside of Manhattan. www.christian-woman-at-the-well.blogspot.com and www.kansas-mornings.blogspot.com

Harley Elliott's books of poetry include *Animals That Stand In Dreams* and *Darkness at Each Elbow*, both available from Hanging Loose Press, Brooklyn, New York, and *The Monkey of Mulberry Pass* and *Loading the Stone*, both from Woodley Press, Topeka, Kansas.

Dennis Etzel Jr. lives with Carrie and their two sons in Topeka, Kansas. He has an MFA in Creative Writing from The University of Kansas and teaches at Washburn University. He is Co-Managing Editor of Woodley Press, Poetry Editor for *seveneightfive*, and hosts the Top City Poetry Reading Series. Work has appeared in *Denver Quarterly, RATTLE, BlazeVOX, kiosk, Poetry Midwest, Coal City Review, Flint Hills Review, I-70 Review,* and *seveneightfive*.

Melissa Fite earned her Master's in English literature from Pittsburg State University in Kansas and now teaches English at Pittsburg High School. She writes poetry as frequently as she can, usually just often enough to keep her from getting kicked out of her beloved workshop group. Melissa lives at home with her boyfriend and dog. www.melissatothefite.blogspot.com.

Amy Fleury is the author of *Beautiful Trouble* (Southern Illinois UP, 2004), and the chapbook, *Reliquaries of the Lesser Saints* (RopeWalk Press,

2010). She was the 2009-10 Amy Clampitt Resident Poetry Fellow. A native of Seneca, Kansas, she now directs the M.F.A. Program at McNeese State University in Louisiana.

Greg German, was born and raised near Glen Elder, Kansas, where he farmed with his family for many years. He has been active within the Kansas literary scene for over 25 years including the development and oversight of www.kansaspoets.com. Currently, with ties to Kansas City, Greg resides with his family on the Caribbean island of Dominica where, amidst many other things, he is involved with country's annual Nature Island Literary Festival. Greg's poetry, all thematically tied to farming and rural Kansas, has appeared in numerous literary journals. Many samples of his writing and photography can be found at www.limestone9.com and www.dominicaliving.com.

Diane Glancy is professor emeritus at Macalester College in St. Paul, MN. She moved to Shawnee Mission, Kansas in 2005. A new collection of essays, *The Dream of a Broken Field*, is forthcoming from the University of Nebraska Press in 2011. Her latest poetry collection, *Stories of the Driven World*, was published by Mammoth Publications. She is the recipient of two National Endowment for the Arts fellowships and an American Book Award. She was born in Kansas City where her father worked for the stockyards.

Katherine Greene lived in ten states and thirty seven houses before settling in Kansas in 1977. She is a writer, a law librarian, a lover of words, and an avid reader. She lives in North Lawrence with her husband in the middle of a beautiful garden and still travels from time to time.

Anne Haehl is a lover of words, both in writing and in storytelling. She lives with her husband of 43 years, three cats and a dog. They have two grown children. She has been published in, among others, *Coal City Review, Studio: a Journal of christians [sic] writing*, and *Chiron Review*. Her chapbook, *Daughter and Mother*, was published by Snark Press in 2004.

Joseph Harrington is the author of *Things Come On: an amneoir* (Wesleyan University Press 2011), *Poetry and the Public* (Wesleyan 2002), and the

chapbook *earth day suite* (Beard of Bees 2010). His creative work also has appeared in *Hotel Amerika, The Collagist, Otoliths, Fact-Simile*, and *P-Queue*, amongst others. He teaches at the University of Kansas in Lawrence.

William J. Harris has published two books of poems, *Hey Fella Would You Mind Holding This Piano a Moment* and *In My Own Dark Way*, a chapbook, *Domande Personali/Personal Questions* and individual poems in more than fifty anthologies of poetry. Currently he is Director of the MFA in the KU English Department.

Serina Allison Hearn, raised in Trinidad and Tobago, studied fashion design at St Martin's School of Art, London, U.K. in the late 70's. Her first book *Dreaming the Bronze Girl* was published by Mid America Press, 2002. *Atlas of Our Birth* was published by Woodley Press, 2010. She currently works in Victorian house restoration in Lawrence, KS. and travels back and forth between latitudes.

Bill Hickok's humorous articles and poems have appeared on the Op-Ed pages of *Cleveland Plain Dealer, The Kansas City Star, Newsday, Philadelphia Enquirer*, and in magazines, such as *Uncle* (for those who have given up), *The Same, I-70*, and online. He is an ornithologist, wildlife photographer, environmentalist, and co-founder of The Writers Place, a literary center in Kansas City. His new book of poetry is *The Woman Who Shot Me* (Whirley Bird Press, 2011).

Steven Hind divides his time between Hutchinson where he taught for three decades and the family farm on the eastern edge of the Flint Hills near Madison. His collection, *The Loose Change of Wonder*, was selected as a 2007 Kansas Notable Book.

Jonathan Holden has been recognized as one of America's foremost poets. He is a University Distinguished Professor of English and Poet-in-Residence at Kansas State University, Manhattan, Kansas, and, in July 2005, was appointed the First Poet Laureate of Kansas. He won numerous awards, published 17 books in addition to more than 190 poems in journals.

Hazel Smith Hutchinson, a SoulCollage® Facilitator (artensoulcollage.com), grew up in

Maine. She began her life in Kansas with her sweet-souled Kansas man 33 years ago. Hazel has been published in *The Flint Hills Review, The Mid America Poetry Review, The Awakenings Review, Animus*, and others.

Nancy Hubble has been a teacher at KU as well as various alternative and public elementary schools. She has had poetry published in the *Lawrence Journal World*, a variety of small zines and a publication by Imagination and Place, *The Wakarusa Wetlands in Word & Image*. Her work includes a CD and chapbook: *Dharma Dog*.

Jennifer Jantz Estes grew up on a farm in the middle of Kansas and spent many summers learning the art of solitude driving a wheat truck across the Great Plains. She writes and works for Eighth Day Books in Wichita, Kansas, but lives (wistful for the prairie) in Canton, Ohio, with her husband, two sons and two dogs.

Judith Bader Jones is a founding member of Whispering Prairie Press, and a poetry editor for *Kansas City Voices*, 2001-2008. Her collection of short fiction, *Delta Pearls* received The William Rockhill Nelson 2007 Fiction Award. Finishing Line Press published *Moon Flowers on the Fence*, June 2010. *The Language of Small Rooms*, a chapbook of poems will be published by Finishing Line Press in 2011. www.judithbaderjones.com.

Kathleen Johnson is the editor and publisher of New Mexico Poetry Review. She received her BFA in history of art and MFA in creative writing from the University of Kansas. As a freelance book critic specializing in poetry, she published over sixty book reviews in *The Kansas City Star* and other publications between 2002 and 2009. Her collection of poems *Burn,* published by Woodley Press in 2008, was selected as a 2009 Kansas Notable Book. A fifth-generation New Mexican, she has divided her time between Kansas and New Mexico for many years. She became a full-time resident of Santa Fe in 2009. www.newmexicopoetryreview.com.

Michael L. Johnson is a professor emeritus from the University of Kansas now living in Santa Fe, New Mexico. His most notable recent book of poems is *Sky Land: A Southwestern Cycle* (Topeka, KS: Woodley Press), which received the 2010 New Mexico Book Award in poetry.

William J. Karnowski is the author of six books including *Pushing the Chain, Painting the Train, Catching the Rain, True Tales Hard Tails and Highways, The Hills of Laclede* and *Dispensation*. He has published over 90 poems in the *Kansas Plus Weekly Capital-Journal Magazine* and numerous websites. Karnowski lives in the Wamego, Kansas, vicinity, near the unincorporated village of Laclede with his wife, Sue. They have three children.

Ken Lassman is the author of *Wild Douglas County* and *Seasons and Cycles: Rhythms of Life in the Kansas Area Watershed*. He writes regularly for *Blue Sky, Green Earth* and has maintained a daily guide to look for what's happening in the natural world, displayed at Z's Divine Espresso, for ten years. He lives on land south of Lawrence, Kansas, where he is fifth generation, and where he restores tallgrass prairie.

Robert N. Lawson is a retired Professor of English at Washburn University, in Topeka, Kansas, where he taught for over thirty years, his specialties Shakespeare and courses in Japanese Literature (with a lot of Freshman Composition in between). He served as General Editor of The Woodley Press from 1980 to 2000.

Philip Kimball is the author of several novels, *Liar's Moon* and *Harvesting Ballads,* and a great deal of poetry, translations and theory. He was born in the first half of the previous century in the front bedroom of a shotgun bungalow two blocks east of downtown Piedmont, Oklahoma, about two miles from the hole in the ground where his paternal grandfather was born (a dugout soddie on the land claimed in the 1889 rush). It was July 21, 1941, on the cusp between Cancer and Leo, the transition from dust bowl, the great depression, to world war and into the atomic age. It was 104°. www.PhilipGKimball.com.

Gary Lechliter's poetry has appeared in Atlanta Review, *Chance of a Ghost: an Anthology of Contemporary Ghost Poems*, Haight Ashbury Literary Journal, New Mexico Poetry Review, Straylight, Tears in the Fence, and Wisconsin Review. He has a recent book, *Foggy Bottoms: Poems about Myths and Legends,* published by Coal City Press.

Stanley Lombardo has published verse translations of Homer's *Iliad* and *Odyssey,* the poems of Sappho, Virgil's *Aeneid*, Ovid's *Metamorphoses,* and Dante's *Inferno.* He teaches Classics at the University of Kansas and, with his wife Judy Roitman, Zen at the Kansas Zen Center.

Katie Longofono is in her third year of undergraduate studies at the University of Kansas. She is pursuing a degree in English with a creative writing emphasis. She is also the founder and lead editor of *Blue Island Review*, a Lawrence-based poetry anthology. Her work has been published in *North Central Review, Kiosk, Blue Island Review,* and *Polyphony Online.* In her spare time she enjoys Scrabble, scarves, and alliteration.

Denise Low, Kansas Poet Laureate 2007-09, is a national board member of the Associated Writing Programs and has awards from the NEH, Lannan, Ks. Arts Commission, and KS Center for the Book. She has taught at Haskell Indian Nations Univ., Univ. of KS and Univ. of Richmond. Her publications include 20 books of poetry and prose. Low grew up in Emporia and is of British, German, Delaware and Cherokee heritage. She is 5th generation Kansan. www.deniselow.com.

Dixie Lubin is a long-time resident of Lawrence, Kansas. She has written for pleasure since she learned to read. She is the author of *Slightly Tilting into the Void* and has had poems in anthologies, including *The Carbon Chronicle-Harvest of Arts Poets 1992-1996, Flatland Press, Lawrence, Kansas* and *Kaw, Kaw, Kaw-as the Poets Fly from Lawrence Kansas,* a CD. Dixie facilitates community writing workshops and writes with incarcerated teens. She is an outsider artist, and a founding mother of the annual "Bizarre Bazaar" in Lawrence.

Jim McCrary was born in Illinois in 1941. He spent the last half of the '60s in Lawrence, the '70s in New York City and San Francisco, the '80s in Sonoma County, and the '90s and oughts back in Lawrence. He won the Pheonix Award from the city of Lawrence for contributions to the literary culture, which was due most to a very successful poetry slam he co-curated at The Flamingo club in North Lawrence. His published books include *West of Mass* from Tansy Press; *All That* from Many Penny Press

and DIY from his own Really Old Gringo Press: *Mental Text* (2010), *My Book* (2009), *Maya Land* (2006), *Holbox* (2006), *Oh Miss Mary* (2001) and *Dive She Said* (2000). His recent work has appeared in the journals *Otoliths* (Australia), *House Organ* (NY) and Galatea Review (CA). His most recent chapbook, *Po Doom,* was published in 2011 by Hanks Orginal Loose Gravel Press.

Ramona McCallum earned her B.A. in creative writing and literature from Kansas State University. Ramona currently lives and writes in Garden City, Kansas where she and her husband, Brian McCallum, are raising their six children. In her spare time, Ramona serves as editor and assistant to her husband, a ceramic sculptor. The couple collaborate on written and visual art projects throughout southwest Kansas.

Jo McDougall lives in Leawood, Kansas. She's Associate Professor Emeritus of English, Pittsburg State University, Pittsburg, Kansas. McDougall is the author of five books of poetry, two chapbooks, and a memoir, *Daddy's Money: a Memoir of Farm and Family* (July 2011, University of Arkansas Press). www.jomcdougall.com

Eric McHenry received the Kate Tufts Discovery Award for his first book of poems, *Potscrubber Lullabies* (Waywiser Press, 2006). Waywiser will publish *Mommy Daddy Evan Sage,* his collection of children's poems with woodcuts by Nicholas Garland, in 2011. McHenry teaches creative writing at Washburn University. www. waywiser-press.com.

Stephen Meats has taught literature and creative writing at Pittsburg State University in Kansas since 1979. He has published poems and short stories in various journals, and his book of poems, *Looking for the Pale Eagle* (1993) was published by Woodley Memorial Press. He has been poetry editor of *The Midwest Quarterly* since 1985.

Lee Mick was raised in Mitchell County, a third generation Kansan, living in Cawker City. He married his wife Denelle in 1978, and is the father of two grown children, Travis and Shawna, and Grandpa to one, so far, little Johnathan. His poetry also appears in the Kansas Authors Club anthology *Tallgrass Voices* published by Hillsong Press.

Ronda Miller moved to Lawrence from NW Kansas where she attained degrees in Creative Writing, University of Kansas. She is a certified Life Coach, graduate of World Company Citizen Journalism Academy and author of *The 150th Pony Express Re-ride*. She writes for *The Examiner*, and created the poetic form, the Loku. Her poetry can be found at *The Smithsonian Institute of Art* and *Tallgrass Voices*. She is the mother of a daughter and a son. www.ljworld.com at random (Ronda Miller – justbegintowrite)

Caryn Mirriam-Goldberg is the poet laureate of Kansas 2009-2012, and the author of over ten books, including four collections of poetry, *The Sky Begins At Your Feet: A Memoir on Cancer, Community and Coming Home to the Body*, and several anthologies. Founder of Transformative Language Arts at Goddard College, where she teaches, she also leads writing workshops widely. With singer Kelley Hunt, Caryn offers Brave Voice writing and singing retreats, collaborative performances and co-written songs. www.CarynMirriamGoldberg.com

Marilyn Pollack Naron, a Chicago native, studied journalism at the University of Kansas, and has enjoyed living in Lawrence for 15 years. A writer, mother and pastry chef, she traded professional baking to write from her own kitchen, now sharing stories, recipes and entertaining ideas on her popular blog Simmer Till Done. She has contributed to The Sister Project and PaulaDeen.com, and is noted by Babble.com as one of the country's "50 Best Mom Food Bloggers."

Rick Nichols penned 51 Burma Shave-like rhymes and a poem, "Messengers," for his book *50 Sermons, 50 States: Presentations from the Pulpit for the People of America*. Residing in an old river house with a good view of Missouri at Leavenworth, he has dubbed himself the "Border Bard." www.borderbard.wordpress.com and www.middleborder.com.

Amy Nixon is an award-winning poet and song-writer who lives in Manhattan, KS with her teenage son and three very spoiled cats. She is passionate about architecture, genealogy, and guacamole, among other things.

Karen Ohnesorge has lived mostly in Kansas

since 1986, having grown up near Oak Ridge, Tennessee— the Atomic City. Her poems have appeared in *Ploughshares*, *The Spoon River Quarterly*, *Mudfish*, *Antioch Review*, and *Chain*. She currently works as Associate Professor of English and Dean of Instruction at Ottawa University in Ottawa, Kansas.

Al Ortolani has been teaching in Kansas for 37 years. His poetry has appeared in the *Midwest Quarterly*, *The English Journal*, *The Laurel Review*, *The New York Quarterly* and others. His second book of poetry *Finding the Edge* was published by Woodley Press in 2011. He is currently co-editor of *The Little Balkans Review*.

H.C. Palmer is a physician who was born in Southeast Kansas and spent much of his time growing up in the Flint Hills, which is his "anchor" place although he considers the Madison Valley in Montana and the Florida Keys as important places too. He lives in Lenexa where he writes poems in his old age.

Dan Pohl grew up across the state of Kansas from Lucas to Lawrence, Americus to Zenda as his father help build I-70 and grain elevators, moving every two years, forever the "new kid." He lives in Moundridge, Kansas and instructs English composition at Hutchinson Community College in Hutchinson, Kansas.

Matthew Porubsky's first book of poetry, *voyeur poems*, published by Coal City Press, was the winner of the Kansas Authors Club Nelson Poetry Book Award in 2006. His second book of poetry, *Fire Mobile (The Pregnancy Sonnets,)* is available from Woodley Memorial Press. He lives in Topeka where he works as a freight conductor for the Union Pacific Railroad. Visit www.mppoetry.com to purchase books and view all other kinds of poetry fun.

Kevin Rabas co-directs the creative writing program at Emporia State University. He has two books of poems, *Bird's Horn* and *Lisa's Flying Electric Piano*, a Kansas Notable Book and Nelson Poetry Book Award winner.

Thomas Reynolds is an associate English professor at Johnson County Community College in Overland Park, Kansas, and has published poems in various print and online journals, including *New Delta Review, Alabama Literary Review, Aethlon-The Journal of Sport Literature, The MacGuffin, Flint Hills Review,* and *Prairie Poetry.* Woodley Press of Washburn University published his poetry collection *Ghost Town Almanac* in 2008.

Linda Rodriguez, born in Fowler, Kansas, has published *Heart's Migration,* winner of the 2010 Thorpe Menn Award for Literary Excellence, and *Skin Hunger.* She received the Inspiration Award from the KC Arts Fund, Elvira Cordero Cisneros Award, Midwest Voices and Visions Award, and both a Ragdale and Macondo Fellowship.

Judith Roitman, born and raised in New York City, landed in Lawrence KS in 1978 after bouncing back and forth between the coasts, and has been here ever since. Her book *No Face: Selected and New Poems* was published by First Intensity Press in 2008. Her work has appeared in a number of journals, including (most recently) *First Intensity, Spectaculum, Locus Point, Delirious Hem,* and *Bird Dog.*

Mark Scheel was born and raised on a farm in rural, east-central Kansas. He served overseas with the American National Red Cross in Vietnam, Thailand, Germany and England and later took graduate studies and taught at Emporia State University. Prior to retirement he was an information specialist with the Johnson County Library in Shawnee Mission, Kansas, and a prose editor for *Kansas City Voices* magazine. His most recent book, *A Backward View: Stories & Poems,* won the J. Donald Coffin Memorial Book Award from the Kansas Authors Club.

Elizabeth Schultz, having retired from the University of Kansas in 2001, now balances scholarship on Herman Melville and on the environment with writing essays and poems about the people and places she loves. She has published two critical works on Melville, two collections of poetry, one book of short stories, and published her scholarship and poetry widely.

Leah Sewell lives in Topeka, Kansas with her two children and husband, Matt. She is the creator and facilitator of the Topeka Writers' Workshop, the features editor of *seveneightfive* magazine, the editor of *XYZ Magazine,* and has

had work published in *Flint Hills Review, Coal City Review, Inscape, Blue Island Review* and other journals.

Melissa Sewell lives in Topeka, Kansas, where she slings coffee and scrubs her daughter's painty fingerprints from the walls. She loves raspberries and being divorced. Her poems have resided in *Susquehanna Review, Inscape, seveneightfive magazine* and *Kansas City Voices.*

William Sheldon lives with his family in Hutchinson, Kansas where he teaches and writes. His poetry and prose have appeared widely in small press publications, including *Columbia, Epoch, Flint Hills Review, Prairie Schooner,* and *Midwest Quarterly.* He is the author of two collections of poetry, *Retrieving Old Bones* (Woodley) and the chapbook *Into Distant Grass* (Oil Hill Press). Mammoth Publications brought out his new collection, *Rain Comes Riding,* in 2011.

Roland Sodowsky worked in Kansas wheat fields as a teenager. His books include *Things We Lose,* an AWP Award Winner for Short Fiction, *Interim in the Desert, Un-Due West.* He received a National Endowment for the Arts Award in 1989 and the National Cowboy Hall of Fame Award for Short Fiction in 1991. His poetry and fiction have also appeared in *Atlantic Monthly, American Literary Review, Glimmer Train,* and *Midwest Quarterly,* among others. A 2009 Kansas Voices winner, he lives with his wife, Laura Lee Washburn, in Pittsburg, KS.

Kim Stafford is the founding director of the Northwest Writing Institute at Lewis & Clark College. He is the author of *The Muses Among Us: Eloquent Listening and Other Pleasures of the Writer's Craft* and *Early Morning: Remembering My Father, William Stafford.*

William Stafford, one of the world's most beloved poets, was born and raised in Kansas, starting his prolific poetic life in Hutchinson in 1914, and going on to receive his BA and MA from the University of Kansas. During the Second World War, Stafford was a conscientious objector and worked in the civilian public service camps-an experience he recorded in the prose memoir *Down My Heart* (1947). He married Dorothy Hope Frantz in 1944; they had four children, including writer Kim Stafford. Stafford taught at Lewis and Clark College from 1948 until 1980. His first major collection of poems, *Traveling Through the Dark,* won the National Book Award in 1963. He went on to publish more than sixty-five volumes of poetry and prose. Among his many honors and awards were a Shelley Memorial Award, a Guggenheim Fellowship, and a Western States Lifetime Achievement Award in Poetry. In 1970, he was the Consultant in Poetry to the Library of Congress (a position currently known as the Poet Laureate).

Mary Stone Dockery's poetry and prose has appeared or is forthcoming in *Gargoyle, Foundling Review, Blood Lotus, Breadcrumb Scabs,* and many other fine journals. In 2011 she received the Langston Hughes Creative Writing Award in Poetry. Currently, she is an MFA student at the University of Kansas in Lawrence, where she teaches English classes and co-edits the *Blue Island Review* and *Stone Highway Review.*

Olive L. Sullivan, an award-winning writer, grew up in Pittsburg, Kansas. Since then, she has lived in cities, mountains, deserts, two foreign countries, and an island, but she returns to Kansas landscapes for the images in her work. She lives with two big dogs and travels every chance she gets.

Mary Swander was appointed Poet Laureate of Iowa in 2009. She is the author of over ten books of poetry and non-fiction. She is a Distinguished Professor of Liberal Arts and Sciences at Iowa State University. Her most recent work is a book of poetry, *The Girls on the Roof* (Turning Point/Word Tech, 2009), a Mississippi River flood narrative.

Patricia Traxler is author of three poetry collections including *Forbidden Words* (Missouri), and has published her poetry widely, including in *The Nation, Ms. Magazine, Ploughshares, Agni, LA Times Literary Supplement, Slate, The Boston Review, and Best American Poetry.* Awards include two Bunting Poetry Fellowships from Radcliffe, Ploughshares' Cohen Award, and a Pablo Neruda Award from *Nimrod.* www.patriciatraxler.com

Roderick Townley, although known primarily as a children's author (*The Great Good Thing, The Door in the Forest, The Blue Shoe,* and others), has published works of criticism and nonfiction, as well as two volumes of poetry: *Three Musicians* (NY: The Smith) and *Final Approach* (VT: The Countryman Press). His honors include the Kansas Governor's Arts Award, a Master Artist Fellowship, the Peregrine Prize for Short Fiction, the Thorpe Menn Award, and two first prizes from the Academy of American Poets. www.rodericktownley.com.

Wyatt Townley is a fourth-generation Kansan. Her work has appeared in journals ranging from *The Paris Review* to *Newsweek.* Books of poetry include *The Breathing Field* (Little, Brown), *Perfectly Normal* (The Smith), and her new collection, *The Afterlives of Trees* (Woodley), completed with a Master Fellowship from the Kansas Arts Commission. www.WyattTownley.com.

Gloria Vando's most recent book, *Shadows and Supposes,* won the Latino Literary Hall of Fame's Book Award and the Alice Fay Di Castagnola Award. She is founding publisher/editor of *Helicon Nine Editions* for which she received the Kansas Governor's Arts Award. In 1992 she and her husband, Bill Hickok, founded The Writers Place, a literary center in Kansas City.

Timothy Volpert, in addition to being a poet, is also a musician, and co-manages Blue Planet Cafe in Topeka. His poems have been published by the wonderful folks at *seveneightfive magazine, Coal City Review, Inscape, Blue Island Review* and more. He loves you, and wants the best for you.

Diane Wahto's poetry has been published in *Midwest Quarterly, AID Review,* and *Coalition Connections: The Feminization of Poverty.* Awards include the American Academy of Poets Award and the 2011 Salina Spring Reading Series New Voice Award. She lives in Wichita, Kansas with her husband and two dogs.

Laura Lee Washburn, director of Creative Writing at Pittsburg State University, is the author of *This Good Warm Place* (March Street) and *Watching the Contortionists* (Palanquin Chapbook Prize). Her poetry has appeared in *Prime Number, Cavalier Literary Couture, Valparaiso Review, The Sun, The Journal,* and elsewhere. Born in Virginia Beach, Virginia, she has lived in Pittsburg since 1997. She is married to the writer Roland

Sodowsky. Laura and Roland host a writing group in Pittsburg that includes Allison Berry, Eric Dutton, Melissa Fite, Olive Sullivan, and Chris Anderson.

Israel Wasserstein was born and raised on the Great Plains and currently teaches at Washburn University in Topeka, KS. He received his MFA from the University of New Mexico in 2006. His poetry and fiction have appeared in *Flint Hills Review, Blue Mesa Review, Coal City Review, BorderSenses* and elsewhere.

Iris Wilkinson lives in North Lawrence just off the banks of the Kaw River. She enjoys leading a creative writing group for the women at the county jail and is thankful for her day job as a college professor at Washburn University.

Donna Lynn Lash-Wolff was born in Las Cruces, New Mexico, but has lived in Kansas most of her life. She works at Kansas University Medical Center and is a Trustee Scholar at Park University. Her writing has appeared in *The Scenic Route,* the *Synapse,* the Kansas City Kansas Community College e-Journal, as part of the Kansas Arts Commission 2010 National Poetry Month *To the Stars* Writing Contest, and as a 2011 Kansas Daily Poem in Your Pocket selection. She is currently compiling her first book of poetry.

Peter Wright, focusing on the shadows that feed and motivate this symphony of existence, has been writing poems for seventeen years. He lives with his partner thirty miles north of Lawrence. As this small stretch of land on a rise in the middle of nowhere is a new arrangement, he looks forward to the continued evolution of his work influenced by the giant whispering Kansas sky. He has self-published one chapbook of short poems called *Spray.*

Pamela Yenser (formerly Pam McMaster) grew up in Wichita. She holds a BA in English (WSU), MA (PSU), and MFA (UI). Yenser was student editor of *Mikrokosmos* and *The Midwest Quarterly Review.* Nominated for AWP and Pushcart Prizes, and recipient of an American Academy of Poets Prize, she teaches college writing in Albuquerque.

Max Yoho, a Topekan and native Kansan, is a retired machinist, and award-winning Kansas author. This poem was originally published in *Felicia, These Fish Are Delicious,* (Dancing Goat Press, 2004). www.dancinggoatpress.com

Editor: Caryn Mirriam-Goldberg

Caryn Mirriam-Goldberg is the Poet Laureate of Kansas from 2009-2012 and the author or editor of over ten books, including four collections of poetry, *Landed* (Mammoth Publications), *Animals in the House* (Woodley Memorial Press), *Reading the Body* (Mammoth Publications) and *Lot's Wife* (Woodley Memorial Press). She also wrote *The Sky Begins At Your Feet: A Memoir on Cancer, Community and Coming Home to the Body* (Ice Cube Press) and a forthcoming novel, *The Divorce Girl*, (Ice Cube Press) and a non-fiction book, *Needle in the Bone: How a Holocaust Survivor and Polish Resistance Righter Beat the Odds and Found Each Other* (Potomac Books). She co-edited with Marilyn L. Taylor, Denise Low and Walter Bargen *An Endless Skyway: Poetry from the State Poets Laureate* (Ice Cube Press), and with Janet Tallman *The Power of Words: A Transformative Language Arts Reader.* Founder of Transformative Language Arts at Goddard College, where she teaches, Dr. Mirriam-Goldberg leads community writing workshops widely, particularly for the cancer community. With Kelley Hunt, she co-writes songs, performs collaboratively and offers "Brave Voice: Writing and Singing for Your Life" workshops and retreats. She is a registered songwriter with B.M.I., and her songs have been performed on *A Prairie Home Campanion* and worldwide by Kelley Hunt. Daily blog: www.CarynMirriamGoldberg.wordpress.com, weekly yoga/writing column: www. TheMagazineOfYoga.com. www.CarynMirriamGoldberg.com and www.BraveVoice.com.

Photographer: Stephen Locke

Stephen Locke is a Director of Photography and professional storm chaser. He produces motion and still photography for for business and private collectors. Based in Kansas City, his Tempest Gallery is a showcase of storm imagery shot throughout the Great Plains. Stephen is also well known for his time-lapse cinematography. Clients include Andrews McMeel Publishing, Accord Publishing, CBS, Mayo Clinic, The Weather Channel, Discovery, Severe Studios, and TornadoVideos.net.

Layout and Design: Leah Sewell and Matthew Porubsky
Leah and Matthew have done book design for Woodley Press, Coal City Press and *seveneightfive* designs titles. For book design inquiries, please email leah.sewell@gmail.com

Begin Again

Acknowledgements

Special thanks to Kevin Rabas and Dennis Etzel Jr. from Woodley Press, and Michael D. Graves and Julie Edmonds for editing assistance. Thanks to Leah Sewell and Matthew Porubsky for book design, Stephen Locke for cover photograph, and all the poets for contributing their work. Most of these poems are published at www.150KansasPoems.wordpress.com.

Abayo Animashaun: "Ode to Bill Stafford" was published in the *Friends of William Stafford Newsletter.*

Jackie Magnuson Ash: a version of "Earthfallen" appeared in *PlainSpoken: Chosen Lives, Chosen Words,* Weary Woman Press, 2000.

Anne Baber: all poems appeared in *Endless,* Georgetown, KY: Finishing Line Press, 2011.
Walter Bargen: "Kansas Freaks" was published in *Laurel Review.*

Roy J. Beckemeyer: "A Kansas Farmwife's Snow Song" was published in the 2011 edition of the *Kansas Authors Club Yearbook* and in *Tallgrass Voices,* Lawrence, KS: Hill Song Press, 2011.

Maril Crabtree: all poetry also appeared in *Moving On,* Columbus, OH: Puddinghouse Press, 2010.

Brian Daldorph: "A Room of My Own" was published in *Jail Time,* Cumbria, UK: Original Plus Press, 2009.

Dennis Etzel: "I Carry Three Birds" was published in *Poetry Midwest.*

Amy Fleury: "Spiritus Mundi" was published in *Reliquaries of the Lesser Saints,* RopeWalk Press, 2010. "Here in Topeka" first appeared in *32 Poems.*

Joseph Harrington: Excerpts of his poems are from *Things Come On: (an amneoir),* Wesleyan University Press, 2011, and *earth day suite,* Beard of Bees, 2010 (free download at: http://beardofbees.com/harrington.html).

William J. Harris: "You Look Beautiful" was published in *Mochila Review: A National Journal.*

Serina Hearn: "Restored Victorian" was published in *Atlas Of Our Birth,* Topeka, KS: Woodley Press, 2010.

Bill Hickok: "Sweet Storm" appeared in *The Woman Who Shot Me,* Whirley Bird Press, 2011.

Nancy Hubble: "Begin Again" appeared in *Dharma Dog,* Lawrence, KS, 2009; "There! There!" was published in *The Wakarusa Wetlands in Word and Image,* Lawrence, KS: Imagination and Place Press, 2005.

Hazel Smith Hutchinson: "With the Knowing" was first published in *The Awakenings Review.*

Kathleen Johnson: All poems published in *Burn,* Topeka, KS: Woodley Press, 2008; "To the Pilgrim Bard, In Gratitude" first appeared in *Westview;* "Frontier Bride" was published in *The Lucid Stone;* "Dust Bowl Diary" was published in *Cottonwood.*

Michael L. Johnson: "Laura Gilpin, The Prairie" was published in *Hermes' Museum: Art Poems,* Santa Fe, NM: Flowerpot Mountain Press, 2010.

Judith Bader Jones: "Farmers" was published in *Moon Flowers on the Fence,* Finishing Line Press, 2010.

Philip Kimball: "Breaking the Plains" appeared in *Phoenix Papers,* Lawrence, KS: Penthe Publishing Co., 1993.

Robert N. Lawson: "Somewhere Near Abilene" was published in *Inscape.*

Stephen Meats: "Night Sounds" was published in the *Flint Hills Review.*

Caryn Mirriam-Goldberg: "Magnolia Tree in Kansas" was published in *Animals in the House,* Topeka, KS: Woodley Press, 2004 and in the *Lawrence Journal-World.*

Thomas Reynolds: "Becoming Pioneers" was published in *Prairie Poetry;* "Immigrant Song" was published in *The Literary Magazine.*

Linda Rodriguez: "Conversation With My Mother's Picture" appeared in *Heart's Migration,* Tia Churcha Press, 2009.

Judith Roitman: "First Muster" appeared in *No Face,* Lawrence, KS: First Intensity Press, 2008.

Mark Scheel: "Rain" originally appeared in *Nostalgia Magazine,* fall/winter 1990 issue. "Prairie Idyl" originally appeared in *Kansas Quarterly,* 1 & 2, 1992.

William Sheldon: All poems in this book are also published in *Rain Comes Riding,* Lawrence, KS: Mammoth Publications, 2011.

Kim Stafford: "Blue Brick" was published in *Prairie Prescription,* Limberlost Press, 2011.

William Stafford: "Assurance" was published with permission from the Estate of William Stafford (thanks to Kim Stafford).

William Sheldon: "The Perfect Poem" first appeared in the *Midwest Quarterly.*

Wyatt Townley: all poems were published in *The Afterlives of Trees,* Topeka, KS: Woodley Press, 2011

Patricia Traxler: "The Call," "First Prairie Winter" and "Cicadas in August" were published in *Forbidden Words,* Columbia, MO, 1993: University of Missouri Press; "Blackberries" appeared in *c: Emily Dickinson Award Anthology,* Universities West Press.

Israel Wasserstein: "Stepping into the Woods" first appeared in Fickle Muses.

Max Yoho: "1942" was originally published in *Felicia, These Fish Are Delicious,* Dancing Goat Press, 2004.